TAX PLANNING FOR EDUCATORS
1987

The American Taxation Association
A Section of the American Accounting Association

KF
6289.8
.E3
T39
1987

Copyright, American Accounting Association
1987, All rights reserved
Library of Congress Catalog Card Number 79-5129
Printed in the United States of America

ISBN: 86539-063-0

American Accounting Association
5717 Bessie Drive
Sarasota, FL 33583

TAX PLANNING FOR EDUCATORS COMMITTEE
AMERICAN TAXATION ASSOCIATION
(1987 Edition)

John O. Everett, Chairman	Virginia Commonwealth University
John B. Barrack	University of Georgia
Jesse V. Boyles	University of Florida
D. Larry Crumbley	Texas A&M University
David M. Maloney	University of Virginia
James P. Trebby	Marquette University
William D. Wallace	University of Mississippi

COMMITTEE ON TAX INFORMATION SERVICE
AMERICAN ACCOUNTING ASSOCIATION
(1973 Edition)

N. Allen Ford, Chairman	University of Kansas
John B. Barrack	University of Georgia
James H. Boyd	Arizona State University
Jesse V. Boyles	University of Florida
John R. Graham	Kansas State University
J. Marion Posey	Touche Ross
Eugene Willis	University of Illinois

COMMITTEE ON TAX INFORMATION
AMERICAN TAXATION ASSOCIATION
(1979 Edition)

Donald H. Skadden, Chairman	University of Michigan
D. Larry Crumbley	Texas A&M University
William L. Raby	Touche Ross
Rod H. Redmond	California State University - Northridge
Allan S. Rosenbaum	Arthur Andersen
Theodore R. Saldin	Washington State University
James E. Wheeler	University of Michigan

CONTENTS

PREFACE vii

CHAPTER I. INTRODUCTION 1
  Purpose of this Report 1
  Fringe Benefits 2
  Tax Concepts and Terminology 4
  The Individual's Formula Illustrated 8

CHAPTER II. RETIREMENT BENEFITS 12
  Basic Retirement Annuity 12
  Other Options for Receipt of Retirement Benefits 14
  Social Security Benefits 15
  Tax-Sheltered Annuities 16
  Faculty Member Who is Also in Business 20
  Deferred Compensation: Professors Employed by
    State and Local Governments 21
  Partial Withdrawal of Investment 22
  Lump-Sum Distributions 22
  Rollovers of Lump-Sum Distributions 26
  Other Types of Retirement Income 27
  Death Benefits 27
  Transfer Tax Considerations - Estate and Gift 28
  Appendix to Chapter II 30

CHAPTER III. INSURANCE PROGRAMS 32
  Group Life Insurance 32
  Medical Insurance 35
  Disability Insurance 37

CHAPTER IV. SCHOLARSHIPS, FELLOWSHIPS AND AWARDS 39
  Scholarships and Fellowships 39
  Grants to Faculty 41
  Tax-Free Scholarships and Fellowships -
    Undesirable Consequences 42
  Prizes and Awards 43

CHAPTER V. TAX CONSEQUENCES OF RELOCATION 45
  Employment-Seeking Expenses 45
  Moving Expenses 46
  Non-Recognition of Gain on Sale of a Residence 53
  Exclusion of Gain on Sale of a Residence 55
  Tax Planning When Moving and Selling a Personal
    Residence 55
  Tax Considerations for a Visiting Professor 56

CONTENTS

CHAPTER VI.   PROFESSIONAL EXPENSES AND REIMBURSEMENTS 61
    Reporting Requirements 61
    Transportation and Travel Expenses 62
    Educational Expenses 67
    Sabbatical Leaves 70
    Attendance at Symposia, Conventions, and Conferences . . 71
    Research Expenses 72
    Home Office 73
    Personal Computers 78
    Miscellaneous Items 79

CHAPTER VII. OTHER FRINGE BENEFITS 82
    Faculty Discounts 82
    Housing 83
    Tuition Plans 84
    Loans to Faculty 85
    Professional Services and Other Fringe Benefits 87
    Reporting of Fringe Benefits 89

PREFACE

In 1973, the American Accounting Association's Committee on Tax Information Service, chaired by Donald H. Skadden, produced a report entitled <u>Faculty Benefits and Tax Planning</u>. This report was published by the American Accounting Association and made available to the public. In 1978, the American Taxation Association, a section of the American Accounting Association, appointed a committee to assume responsibility of updating that report. The Committee on Tax Information, chaired by N. Allen Ford, published the revised report in 1979 under the title <u>Tax Planning for Educators</u>.

In 1985, the American Taxation Association appointed a new committee to update the 1979 publication. This volume, which incorporates the provisions of the Tax Reform Act of 1986, represents the efforts of that committee.

> John O. Everett
> Committee Chairman
> Richmond, Virginia
> January, 1987

CHAPTER I

INTRODUCTION

The United State Congress has for many years, and in many ways, encouraged employers to adopt various employee benefit programs as supplements to the normal salary and wage income. It has long been considered socially desirable for employers to provide their employees with such things as retirement benefits, insurance coverage, medical plans, and other fringe benefits to improve the quality of life of the average American family. These various benefits, provided primarily through the private sector of the economy, are indispensable augmentations to the many social welfare programs provided by the government.

University faculties and administrators have realized for some time that the rationale for supplemental benefits applies to not-for-profit institutions in much the same way that it applies to profit motivated enterprises. Faculty members and their families seek the same types of security and protection as do other individuals. The advantages to the employer in promoting employee efficiency, contentment, and stability are just as important in educational institutions as elsewhere. It thus seems important that professors and administrators alike understand the fringe benefits that are being, or might be, made available to faculty members.

Entirely apart from the fringe benefit area, Congress, the Treasury Department and the Courts have adopted a myriad of provisions that relate to employees and professional persons in general and, in some instances, to faculty members in particular. These relate to the proper reporting of income and expense items for income tax purposes. Presumably each of these provisions was introduced either to improve equity among taxpayers or to furnish a desirable refinement in the computation of taxable income.

In our self-assessment system, all taxpayers, including faculty members, are expected and encouraged to utilize properly the many legislative, administrative and judicial provisions in the annual computation of their tax liability. Furthermore, it is entirely proper for taxpayers to plan their financial affairs in such a manner as to avail themselves of the various benefits provided in the overall tax structure.

Purpose of This Report

In light of the benefits of tax planning, this report is intended to help faculty members and school administrators in several ways:

(1) Identify and describe various fringe benefit programs which seem to be applicable to the academic situation.
(2) Indicate in some instances the frequency with which some of the programs are being utilized by colleges and universities.
(3) Describe some specific provisions included in some of the benefit programs.
(4) Explain many tax provisions relating to income and deduction items that are particularly relevant to the faculty members.
(5) Discuss some of the ways that the school and the professor can facilitate the minimization of the faculty member's tax liability.

Fringe Benefits

While many fringe benefits are common to employees of both profit oriented and not-for-profit institutions, some tax-free fringe benefits such as profit sharing plans are not pertinent to the academic situation. However, only employees of educational and some other exempt organizations are entitled to certain "tax sheltered annuity" features as described in the Retirement Benefits section. While profit-oriented entities are concerned with the availability of a deduction for any cost of providing fringe benefits, educational institutions do not share that concern.

Although studies related to the nature and frequency of fringe benefit programs do exist, there is at present a shortage of current material with respect to this topic. A 1980 publication entitled Benefit Plans in Higher Education provides a great deal of descriptive and statistical information about these fringe benefit programs.[1]

The American Association of University Professors publishes an annual survey of faculty salaries which includes some information regarding fringe benefits which can be measured in monetary terms. The AAUP was very cooperative and helpful in providing the information in Table 1 which pertains to 2,159 public and private universities and colleges which responded to a comprehensive salary survey questionnaire. The 1985-1986 AAUP summary indicates that the fringe benefits averaged 22 percent of salary for all ranks combined.

---

[1] King, Francis P., and Cook, Thomas J., Benefit Plans in American Colleges, Columbia University Press, 1980.

TABLE I

AVERAGE FRINGE BENEFITS AS A PERCENTAGE OF SALARY,
BY AFFILIATION AND ITEMIZED BENEFITS, 1985-86

Itemized Benefits	All Combined	Public	Private Independent	Church-Related
Retirement	9.7	10.5	8.5	6.8
Medical Insurance	4.1	4.3	3.5	3.8
Disability Income	.3	.3	.3	.4
Tuition	.8	.2	2.1	2.3
Dental Insurance	.2	.2	.1	.1
Social Security	5.7	5.4	6.1	6.6
Unemployment Compensation	.3	.2	.4	.5
Life Insurance	.3	.3	.5	.4
Workmen's Compensation	.4	.4	.4	.4
Benefits in Kind (Moving, Housing, etc.)	.3	.2	.8	.3
All Combined	22.1	22.0	22.7	21.6

Source: "The Annual Report on the Economic Status of the Profession," Academe: Bulletin of the American Association of University Professors, Vol. 72, No. 5 (September - October, 1986), p. 13.

Tax Concepts and Terminology

The Tax Reform Act (TRA) of 1986 represents the most far-reaching and fundamental revision of the United States income tax in its history. A process that began with a goal of simplification eventually produced a 925-page bill which added several layers of complexity to the tax system.

In general, the lower tax rates of this "revenue neutral" bill were made possible only by a broadening of the individual tax base. Educators were not immune to this restructuring of the definition of taxable income; for example, the rules allowing noncandidates for a degree to excluded limited amounts of research grants were repealed. In addition, several modifications in the reporting of unreimbursed employee expenses will adversely affect most educators.

A thorough discussion of the revised tax reporting procedures for all taxpayers is beyond the scope of this work. However, it may prove beneficial to review a few basic tax concepts and terminology before looking at the specific rules affecting educators.

<u>Gross Income</u>   The normal starting point for computing one's tax liability is first to determine total gross income. Gross income includes all income from whatever source derived except for amounts which are specifically excluded. Items which are excluded from gross income, i.e., "exclusions," represent income which is not subject to taxes. Interest on state and municipal securities, life insurance proceeds, and certain scholarships are examples of items which are excluded from gross income by statute. (Several popular exclusions, such as the $100 dividends exclusion ($200 on a joint return) were repealed by the Tax Reform Act of 1986.) As mentioned earlier, Congress has specifically excluded certain employee fringe benefits from gross income such as employer contributions for qualified retirement plans, accident and health plans, group term life insurance and group legal services plans. Since fringe benefits such as the above are not included in gross income, employers are often able to provide considerable additional compensation without incurring significant costs.

While certain fringe benefits are specifically excluded from gross income, most employees receive other fringe benefits which are not taxed for various reasons including custom and difficulties associated with measuring the benefits. While many might readily agree that a professor's free use of the college tennis courts or a corporate employee's free use of the company's gymnasium constitute income, most people would also acknowledge the difficulty of measuring such benefits. Of course, many employees receive "psychic" benefits where measurement is virtually impossible. In recent years, Congress has attempted to clarify the tax treatment of many of these fringe benefits. For example, the 1986 Act contains very specific rules regarding the taxation of campus housing provided to a faculty member.

Deductions for Adjusted Gross Income. Once gross income is ascertained, the taxpayer reduces gross income by various deductions in order to determine taxable income. Note that deductions reduce gross income whereas exclusions are not included in gross income. If an expenditure is found to be deductible, it is necessary to classify it as either being deductible for the determination of adjusted gross income or from adjusted gross income. After adjusted gross income is computed by subtracting from gross income those deductions for adjusted gross income, it is reduced by deductions from adjusted gross income, i.e., personal exemption deductions and the larger of a standard deduction or total itemized deductions.

Deductible expenditures include those related to a trade or business; production of income; management, conservation, or maintenance of property held for the production of income; the determination, collection, or refund of any tax; and certain personal expenses. An employee such as a teacher may deduct all qualifying ordinary and necessary expenses related to the teaching profession.

To determine adjusted gross income, employees may deduct from gross income only those business expenses which are reimbursed by the employer. Prior to 1987, employees were also allowed to deduct for adjusted gross income any unreimbursed transportation and overnight business travel costs. These expenses are now treated as miscellaneous itemized deductions, the total of which is deductible only to the extent that it exceeds 2 percent of adjusted gross income.

Other deductions used to compute adjusted income are alimony payments, expenditures related to the production of rent and royalty income regardless of whether the activity constitutes a trade or business, contributions to a Keogh plan, certain contributions to an Individual Retirement Account, and certain losses due to the sale or exchange of assets. Prior to 1987, a taxpayer was also allowed to deduct 60 percent of any long-term gain on the sale of a capital asset. This deduction was repealed by the Tax Reform Act of 1986; however, for 1987 only, a taxpayer may elect to pay an alternative 28% tax rate on any net long-term capital gain.

Deductions From Adjusted Gross Income.

Deductions from adjusted gross income are divided into two categories: (1) personal exemption deductions and (2) the larger of a standard deduction or total itemized deductions. Personal exemption deductions are available for a taxpayer, his or her spouse, and any qualifying dependents. The amount of each personal exemption deduction is $1,900 in 1987, $1,950 in 1988, and $2,000 in 1989 and later years.

The standard deduction has changed frequently over the years and is affected by the taxpayer's filing status. For example, the 1988 standard deduction is $3,000 for a single person, $4,400 for a head of household, $5,000 for married taxpayers filing a joint return and certain "surviving spouses", and $2,500 for married taxpayers filing separate returns. (For 1987 only, these amounts are set at $2,540, $2,540, $3,760, and $1,880, respectively.) Prior to 1987, the standard deduction was incorporated into the tax rate schedules as a "zero bracket amount." As a consequence, taxpayers who itemized their deductions in those years would deduct only the excess of total itemized deductions over the zero bracket amount.

Some expenditures which are treated as itemized deductions are medical expenses, interest, charitable contributions, taxes, casualty losses, and moving expenses. The category of "miscellaneous itemized deductions" (subject to a 2 percent of adjusted gross income floor) includes union dues, fees to determine one's tax liability and any unreimbursed employee business expenses. Such items as the cost of professional journals, professional dues, special clothing and supplies are typical employee business expenses. Taxpayers normally will itemize deductions if itemized deductions exceed the appropriate standard deduction. When itemized deductions are less than the standard deduction, the taxpayer does not receive any tax benefit for those itemized deductions. Thus, a professor who is single does not receive any tax benefit for the cost of a professional journal if his or her other total itemized deductions are less than $3,000 in 1988 ($2,540 in 1987). For purposes of tax planning, this is an extremely significant point.

When an employer reimburses the employee for an employee business expense, e.g., pays the first $50 of the cost of subscribing to professional journals, the reimbursed portion of the employee business expenses is treated as a deduction for adjusted gross income. As previously discussed, an employee who does not itemize deductions and incurs employee business expenses such as professional dues receives no tax benefit from the expenditure for the dues. Such an employee would be benefited substantially if his or her employer adopted a reimbursement policy for employee business expenses which are otherwise deducted only from adjusted gross income. Such a policy would also shield the reimbursed expenditure from the adverse effects of the 2 percent floor on miscellaneous itemized deductions. At this point it might be appropriate to note that if the employer is willing to reimburse the employee for certain expenditures and the employee who incurs such expenses does not request reimbursement, no deduction is allowed.

<u>Determining the Net Tax Liability</u>. After deriving taxable income, the taxpayer's filing status must be determined. Married taxpayers almost always find it advantageous to file a joint return. After the death of one of the taxpayers, the surviving spouse may be eligible to use joint return rates for two years after the year of death if certain conditions are satisfied. Other unmarried taxpayers may be eligible to file as head of household which is more desirable than filing as a single person. Since it is more advantageous to file as single instead of married filing separately, a married person who has been abandoned by his or her spouse should be alert to the possibility of being treated as unmarried for tax purposes.

Tax credits, which result in a direct reduction of the tax liability, have been increasing in number during the last few years. Since from an equity standpoint tax credits are more desirable than tax deductions, it will not be surprising to see the list of tax credits expanded in the near future. While a tax deduction is more beneficial for one in a high tax bracket as opposed to someone subject to a lower tax rate, a tax credit is equally beneficial to both taxpayers. Most tax credits are directly related to business activities. Prior to 1986, employees such as teachers were sometimes entitled to an investment tax credit (ITC) when they acquired tangible depreciable property for use in their business as an employee. This credit was repealed by the 1986 Act.

A number of credits are available only to individual taxpayers. The earned income credit is unique since it represents the only refundable credit; taxpayers with earned income or adjusted gross income of $14,500 ($17,000 for tax years beginning after 1987) or more are not eligible for this credit. A retired person who is 65 or older may be entitled to a tax credit for the elderly and even taxpayers under 65 who retire because of a permanent disability may be entitled to a credit.

When the IRS does not agree with the taxpayer's determination of his or her tax liability for reason other than math mistakes, the taxpayer has numerous opportunities to settle the disagreement without going to court. While most taxpayers probably prefer to avoid litigation, it is now possible for taxpayers to utilize the small claims division of the Tax Court if litigation is necessary. The amount of tax in dispute must not exceed $10,000. Taxpayers pay a modest filing fee and may present their own case since formal rules of evidence are relaxed. However, the taxpayer may not appeal the decision and it may not be used as a precedent in other cases.

The Individual's Formula Illustrated

At this point, it may prove beneficial to illustrate the individual tax computation. The following example presents the tax formula under both 1986 and 1987 tax laws, highlighting the changes instituted by The Tax Reform Act of 1986. Many of these changes affecting educators are explained in detail in succeeding chapters.

The net effect of tax reform on individual taxpayers depends on their "mix" of income, deductions, and credits. Although the net tax liability of the taxpayers in the example increased by $340 under the 1987 law, the lower tax rates of 1988 will generate a net tax liability of $1,180, which is $211 less than 1986 law.

ILLUSTRATION OF THE 1986 AND 1987 TAX FORMULAS

Bill and Mary Adams, both age 38, are married taxpayers who file a joint income tax return for the current tax year. They provide all of the support of their two minor children.

Bill is a professor at State University. He earned a salary of $42,000 during the current year ($2,000 of which was deferred in a tax shelter annuity) and received $4,200 of royalty income from a textbook on which he is a coauthor. His cash expenses related to the textbook totaled $1,400, and his allowable home office deduction totals $600. Bill acquired a personal computer during the year which will be used soley for the textbook and consulting work. The total cost was $3,000.

Mary joined the faculty at State University in June of the current year. Her salary for the remainder of the year was $18,200. For the first five months of the year, she was a Ph.D. candidate at Local University. During this time she received $1,000 compensation for teaching one class during the year (all candidates for the Ph.D. degree are required to teach one class a year).

Bill and Mary's other income during the year consisted of the following: $1,200 interest on certificates of deposit, $900 dividends on ABC Corporation stock, a $500 teaching award won by Mary as the outstanding faculty member in the college, a $1,500 summer research grant received by Bill from the National Science Foundation for post-graduate work (payable $500 a month for 3 months), and $1,000 received from the sale of 50 shares of ABC stock (acquired in 1983 for $600).

Bill and Mary's legitimate expenses for the year include:

```
$2,000 contributed by Bill to an I.R.A.
 1,200 contributions to qualified charities
   900 property taxes on personal residence
 2,000 state income taxes
   300 state and local sales taxes
 2,400 interest expense (includes $400 consumer interest)
   320 professional dues and subscriptions
    80 cost of preparing last year's tax returns
    50 unreimbursed expenses of entertaining faculty recruit
   200 unreimbursed travel expenses (to convention)
    50 unreimbursed registration fee at convention
    50 contribution to Democratic party
 9,300 total federal income tax withholdings and prepayments
```

	1986 LAW	1987 LAW
Gross Income:		
Gross Salary - Bill (net of deferral)	$40,000	$40,000
Gross Salary - Mary	18,200	18,200
Ph.D. Teaching Compensation - Mary	0	1,000a
Textbook Income - Bill	4,200	4,200
Interest Income	1,200	1,200
Dividend Income 900		900
Less Exclusion (200)		(0)b
	700	900
Teaching Award - Mary	0	500c
Summer Research Grant - Bill 1,500		1,500
Less Exclusion ($300 month) (900)		(0)d
	600	1,500
Gain on Sale of Stock (Gross)	400	400
Gross Income	$65,300	$67,900
Deductions For AGI:		
Textbook Expenses - Bill:		
Cash Expenses 1,400		1,400
Home Office Deduction 600		600
Depreciation - Computer 428e		600f
Capital Gain Deduction (60%) 240		- g
Unreimbursed Travel Expense 200		- h
Two-Earner Deduction 1,820		- i
I.R.A. Contribution 2,000		- j
	(6,688)	(2,600)
Adjusted Gross Income (AGI)	$58,612	$65,300

a - All required degree services are now taxable
b - Dividend exclusion is repealed, effective 1987
c - In general, all awards will be taxable beginning in 1987
d - Scholarship exclusion for noncandidates repealed in 1987
e - ($3,000 cost - $150 ITC adjustment) x .15 ACRS factor
f - ($3,000 cost) x .20 ACRS factor
g - Long-term capital gains taxed in full; 60% deduction repealed
    (However, the $400 gain is taxed at a flat 28% rate)
h - All employee expenses moved to itemized deductions (subject
    to 2% of adjusted gross income floor)
i - Two-earner deduction for working married coupled repealed
j - Since AGI exceeds $50,000, no I.R.A. deduction is allowed

(CONTINUED ON NEXT PAGE)

	1986 LAW	1987 LAW
Adjusted Gross Income	$58,612	$65,300

Deductions From AGI:			
Personal Exemptions (4)		(4,320)	(7,600)k
Itemized Deductions:			
Contributions	$1,200		$1,200
State & Local Taxes (Sum)	3,200		2,900l
Interest Expense	2,400		2,260m
Miscellaneous Expenses:			
Dues & Subscriptions	320		320
Tax Return Fees	80		80
Unreimbursed Entertainment	50		40n
Unreimbursed Registration	50		50
Unreimbursed Travel	-		200o
Less 2% of AGI			(690)p
Total Itemized Deductions	7,300		6,360
Less Zero-Bracket Amount	(3,670)		- q
		(3,630)	(6,360)
Taxable Income		$50,662	$51,340
Gross Tax Liability		$11,016	$11,031
Less: Investment Tax Credit		(300)	- r
Political Credit		(25)	- s
Withholdings		(9,300)	(9,300)
Net Tax Liability		$ 1,391	$ 1,731

k - Personal exemption amounts increased to $1,900 each in 1987
l - State and local sales tax deduction repealed in 1987
m - Of the $400 consumer interest, 35%, or $140, is disallowed
n - Only 80% of qualifying entertainment expense is deductible
o - All unreimbursed employee expenses are now itemized deductions
p - Total miscellaneous itemized ($690) are less than 2% of AGI ($1,306); therefore, none are deductible
q - The zero-bracket amount is no longer in the tax tables
r - The investment tax credit is repealed, effective 1-1-86
s - The political contributions credit is repealed after 1986

1988 Results:
   Using the 1988 tax rates and revised figures for exemptions and interest expense, the net tax liability would be $1,180.

CHAPTER II

RETIREMENT BENEFITS

Retirement plans vary significantly among colleges and universities. Under some plans the employer matches an employee's contribution to the plan; under others, the employer pays more than a matching contribution. In a few colleges, the employer pays the entire contribution to the plan. A faculty member may be eligible to join a retirement plan on the first day of employment, although a waiting period is required by some institutions. An employer's contribution towards a retirement annuity may vest (become the property of the faculty member) immediately. Alternatively, the contribution may be forfeitable until the faculty member has been employed by the college a specified number of years. Some plans are funded; others carry an unfunded obligation of the employer.

Certain plans provided for employees of state-funded institutions cover both faculty members and other state employees, while other state plans cover faculty under a separate retirement system. Many plans guarantee retirement benefits equal to a percentage of the average salary earned by a faculty member during various time periods. Other plans provide whatever benefit can be paid by the funds invested in the plan on the faculty member's behalf. Some plans integrate their payroll deductions closely with Social Security. For those plans which are integrated, the increasing Social Security base has resulted typically in a decline in the value of the commercial annuity provided under the plan.

This section will explain the tax aspects of certain types of retirement benefits. The reader who is interested in the characteristics of the Teachers Insurance and Annuity Association of America (TIAA) and College Retirement Equities Fund (CREF) system should see Appendix A of this section. Appendix A is designed to present, as a point of reference, some information on the largest retirement system available to colleges and universities.

Basic Retirement Annuity [1]

The usual retirement annuity contract provides the annuitant with a stream of monthly benefit payments. In tax-qualified annuity plans the employer's contribution to the plan is not

---

[1] Internal Revenue Code of 1986 (IRC), Sec. 72

considered to be taxable income for the employee at the time of the contribution. Instead, it is taxed when the employee retires and receives monthly benefits. Any earnings accumulated on the contributions are not taxed until distributed to the annuitant. Since retired individuals are usually subject to lower tax rates, a tax-qualified retirement annuity can provide the annuitant with considerably more after-tax dollars than a non-tax-qualified plan.

Employees also may contribute to a tax-qualified annuity plan, and in most instances, these contributions are not deductible by the employee. When the employee later receives the retirement benefits, the portion attributable to the employee's after-tax contribution is received tax-free. This treatment follows logically since income taxes have already been paid on the contributions at the time they were earned and contributed.

To illustrate the normal situation, assume that a male or female faculty member (FM) has contributed $14,000 to a retirement annuity contract while employed. FM's employer, the university, has contributed $14,001 (in order to distinguish the two figures in this discussion). When FM retires at age 65, the funds accumulated to his or her credit are:

FM's investment (already taxed)	$14,000
University contributions (not taxed when contributed)	14,001
Earnings accumulated through the years (not yet taxed)	17,000
Total value of FM's contract	$45,001

FM is to receive monthly retirement benefits. If FM is a 65-year old male, government tables indicate that he should have an expected remaining life of 15 more years.[2] This expected life must be used for income tax purposes. If a contract value of $45,001 will enable him to receive $400 per month for the rest of his life (a single life annuity), his "expected return" will be $72,000 (15 x $4,800).

The tax treatment of this annuity takes into account his investment in the annuity of $14,000 and his "expected return" of $72,000. Thus, for each dollar he receives after retirement, 14/72 is considered to be a return of his investment and, therefore, is not taxable. Assuming that he and his wife, who is less than 65 years of age, have no other income and file a joint return, the tabulation below shows that no federal income tax

---

[2] Reg. Sec. 1.72-9

would be paid under current law.

　　Retirement Benefits

Annual benefits	$4,800	
Excluded portion, (14/72 x $4,800)	933	
Taxable portion		$3,867

Less:

Exemptions for himself at $1,900 (in 1987)	$1,900	
Exemption for his wife	$1,900	
Standard deduction (1987)	$3,760	$7,560
Taxable income		$ -0-
Federal income tax		$ -0-

　　The law permits FM to exclude 14/72 of any amounts received, until he has received the total amount he contributed (beyond age 80). If he fails to survive that long, the unrecovered amount may be claimed as a deduction in FM's final taxable year.

Other Options for Receipt of Retirement Benefits

　　If FM chooses a single life annuity as in the example above, the annuity benefits will cease when he dies. Depending upon the financial resources available to his spouse after his death, FM may not want to select a single life annuity and risk leaving his wife with a substantially diminished income after his death. Therefore, other options need to be examined.

　　FM might choose an option which pays lesser benefits each month, in order to provide monthly benefits for the survivor (either FM or his spouse). An example of this option would be a survivor annuity with a ten-year guarantee period and a two-thirds benefit to the survivor. Some assumed results are used below to compare this option with the single life annuity.

	Single Life Annuity	Two-thirds to Survivor with 10-year Guarantee
Benefits per month, while both are living, FM is 65, spouse is 62 when FM retires	$400.00	$344.00

14

```
        Benefits per month, to the
          spouse after FM dies
          (assume FM dies first)           $ -0-          $229.33
                                                        (two-thirds)
        If both die within the
          first ten years, benefits
          to beneficiary or beneficiaries
          for the remainder of the ten-
          year period.                     $ -0-          $229.33
```

   FM will probably find that his plan has a number of other alternative options for receiving benefits. For example, he may be able to select a joint life and survivor annuity plan with monthly benefit payments after either spouse dies equal to the monthly payments received while both are living. For their ages of 65 and 62, the Internal Revenue Service tables indicate a probability of 23.5 years of benefit payments. Because payments can be expected to be made for 23.5 years, rather than the 15 years for a single life annuity, the monthly benefit payment will be somewhat less than $400.

   If FM is not satisfied with any of the preceding options, he might choose a joint life annuity in which the survivor's benefits would be 50 percent of the monthly benefits received while both were living. One may use a plan which contains a provision guaranteeing that the total accumulation in the fund on the date FM retired would be paid to him or his beneficiaries. This is termed a refund feature. When a plan contains a refund feature an adjustment must be made to compute the exclusion ratio; this adjustment is explained in Treas. Regs. 1.72-7.

Social Security Benefits

   Most faculty members are eligible to receive non-taxable Social Security benefits when they retire. To be eligible to receive benefits, a faculty member must have worked a certain number of calendar quarters and paid Social Security taxes on a changing amount of wages during each quarter. The number of calendar quarters needed to qualify for benefits varies depending upon the year in which the faculty member attains age 65 (but never more than 40 quarters).

   The amount of retirement income a faculty member will receive from Social Security is dependent on several variables. The average amount of covered compensation earned over a period of years is probably the most important factor. Other variables include age at the time benefits are first received, the number of years the faculty member pays into Social Security, and the amount of income earned during the years benefits are being received. Social Security checks will not be affected by earnings after the faculty member attains age 70.

The spouse of a living faculty member may receive benefits as a retired working person or as a spouse of a retired employee. The spouse is entitled to the higher of the two types of benefits, but not both. Unless the spouse earns at a fairly high level, benefits paid to the spouse as a retired working person might not exceed the benefits attributable to the spouse of a retired employee. This seemingly unfair result occurs even though as a working couple they would pay more in Social Security taxes than if only one spouse worked.

If the primary wage earner dies, the surviving spouse may receive survivors benefits. Disability benefits may be received when an employee is disabled. Certain dependents of the employee also may receive benefits because of the employee's disability. Eligibility requirements for disability and survivors benefits differ from the requirements for retirement benefits.

The Social Security system is funded by Social Security taxes. The taxes are computed by multiplying a flat rate times an earnings base. The data applicable to employees for years 1986 and 1987 is as follows:

	Rate	Earnings Base	Maximum Employee Tax
1986	7.15	$42,000	3,003.00
1987	7.15	$43,800	3,131.70

Taxpayers should check once every three or four years with the Social Security Administration to verify the accuracy of their earnings record. A postcard form OAR-7004, "Request for Statement of Earnings" as well as information about Social Security may be obtained from a local Social Security office.

Tax-Sheltered Annuities[3]

A university or college professor is eligible to participate in a tax-sheltered annuity. Under Section 403(b) the professor will not be taxed currently on the amount the employer invests for him in a tax-sheltered annuity, provided the amounts invested do not exceed certain limitations provided by the Code. The amounts invested will be taxed as ordinary income when withdrawn from the

---

[3] IRC Sec. 403(b) and Reg. Sec. 1.403(b)

plan at a later date. In addition, interest and dividends accumulated on these amounts will be tax-free to the professor until subsequently received. This allows "pre-tax" dollars to earn tax deferred income for a period of years. Note that these pre-tax dollars are dollars that would otherwise have been taxed at the professor's highest marginal tax rate in the year they were "earned."

In practice, most tax-sheltered annuities are funded indirectly by the professor through a procedure termed "salary reduction." This procedure permits the professor to take a reduction in salary (or to forego an increase in salary), and to have this amount contributed by the employer toward the purchase of a tax-sheltered annuity. Since most tax-sheltered annuities are supplementary to a regular retirement plan, the employer normally does not match these amounts.

The tax savings generated by a tax-sheltered annuity funded through salary reduction can be illustrated by an example. Assume FM earns $25,000 annually from his job as a professor. Under a salary reduction arrangement, she agrees to accept a salary of $24,000 with the understanding that the employer will contribute $1,000 to a tax-sheltered annuity. Neither the $1,000 invested by the employer in the annuity nor any interest or dividends generated by the $1,000 will be taxed to FM currently. Taxes will be paid when these funds are withdrawn from the plan. However, the present-value cost of those future tax payments is likely to be much less than the current tax that would have to be paid.

The tax law imposes three limitations on the amount an employee may "shelter" through tax-sheltered annuity plans. Amounts invested in such plans cannot exceed several limitations. The annual limitation restricts the maximum annual investment to the smaller of 25 percent of the employee's compensation or $30,000 for the year less certain amounts including any current contribution to the TSA by the employer. For example, if FM's annual salary is $25,000, the annual limitation is $5,000 [($25,000-$5,000) x 25%].

A second limitation, the exclusion allowance, is somewhat more complex. The following steps will enable one to compute this limitation:

(1) Determine one's salary net of any amounts contributed to a tax-sheltered annuity through a salary reduction arrangement.

(2) Multiply the reduced salary computed in (1) by 20%.

(3) Multiply the amount obtained in (2) by the number of years employed by the current employer.

(4) Sum all the amounts that have been contributed by the current employer to both the tax-sheltered annuity and the employer's qualified defined contribution retirement plan.

(5) The exclusion allowance limitation is satisfied if (3) exceeds (4).

To illustrate, assume again that FM's annual salary is $25,000, and that his employer contributes $3,000 to a tax-sheltered annuity under a salary reduction arrangement. In prior years, only $1,000 had been contributed annually to the plan. FM's annual salary has increased by $2,000 each year since he started working for his current employer four year ago. FM's employer contributes an amount equal to six percent of his regular salary to a pension plan. FM has been a participant in both the pension plan and the tax-sheltered annuity during all four years. The overall limitation would be computed as follows:

(1) Salary net of contributions to the tax-sheltered annuity = $22,000

(2) $22,000 x 20% = $4,400

(3) $4,400 x 4 = $17,600

(4) .06 ($25,000 + $23,000 + $21,000 + $19,000) + $3,000 + $1,000 + $1,000 + $1,000 = $11,280

(5) The exclusion allowance limitation is satisfied since $17,600 exceeds $11,280

After 1986 there is a $9,500 limitation on all *elective* employee deferrals to a tax-sheltered annuity (or a 403(f) plan). This third limitation applies *only* to elective employee deferrals and does not apply to employer contributions. The law is unclear whether matching contributions by a faculty member as a condition of employment are elective deferrals.

Four extraordinarily complex exceptions exist to these three rules, which may permit certain faculty to increase further their participation in a tax-sheltered annuity.[4] If one wishes to participate more fully in a tax-sheltered annuity, these exceptions should be examined. Fortunately, the employer and insurance agent should be trained to determine these maximum amounts. Therefore, they will not be discussed in this report.[5]

Several types of tax-sheltered annuities exist. The most common is the annuity which provides a fixed rate of return. Virtually all companies selling tax-sheltered annuities have fixed-rate plans. Some companies sell annuities which permit participation in a bond or stock fund. The amount contributed plus the earnings of the fund will determine the size of the annuity available. Some companies do not permit withdrawals from the annuity fund until the employee retires. Others allow faculty members to withdraw annuity funds at any time. Certain of the companies permitting pre-retirement withdrawals limit the amount of the withdrawals and/or require a penalty to be paid on the amounts withdrawn.

Considerable financial flexibility can be obtained by investing in annuities which permit early withdrawals. For example, a faculty member might want to save to buy a home, or to finance a child's higher education. Accordingly, he or she might invest $300 per year for 15 years, with the amount accumulated to be withdrawn during the child's college years. Inasmuch as he or she would pay no income tax on the $300 invested each year, the dollars he or she would have paid in tax are available to work for the professor throughout that time. These additional "tax" dollars invested in the annuity can increase substantially the amount available for the child's education. By withdrawing amounts from the annuity in years when one has reduced income, the tax-sheltered annuity may also be used to smooth one's taxable income. However, after March 15, 1987, there is a 10 percent tax on early withdrawal from a tax-sheltered annuity. The penalty tax is 10 percent of the taxable portion of the distribution that is

---

[4] IRC Secs. 415(e)(4) and 402(g)(8)

[5] For more detail, see Crumbley, Apostolou, and Wiggins, "Tax-Sheltered Plans in Educational and Other Organizations," The CPA Journal, April, 1984, pp. 22-31. Schnee and Caldwell, "Retirement Planning Under Section 403(b)(7): Advantages and Limitations," The Journal of the American Taxation Association, Fall, 1984, pp. 48-56. Hira, "Tax-Sheltered Annuities: A Topic Ignored by Professionals," Journal of Pension Planning & Compliance, December, 1984, pp. 439-454

attributable to employer contributions and the amount representing after-tax employee contributions and matching contributions. The penalty is not deductible.

Not all faculty members will be in a financial position which enables them to invest in a tax-sheltered annuity. Some people may find a tax-sheltered annuity most feasible towards the end of their working career when their salaries are higher and their living costs lower. A faculty person who has access to other income (royalties, consulting fees, summer pay, spouse's income), is often in an excellent position to invest large amounts in a tax-sheltered annuity.

Faculty Member Who is Also in Business

A faculty member may have independent business income, perhaps from consulting fees or from book royalties. This outside income will qualify him or her to establish a self-employment retirement plan as an adjunct to his or her university plan. Such plans are particularly valuable if one of the tax-sheltered savings plans is not available through the university to skim off the top portion of his or her salary.[6]

Self-employment retirement plans are popularly referred to as Keogh plans. Most Keogh plans are administered by a bank or savings and loan association, although Keogh contributions may be used to purchase annuity contracts or special government retirement bonds. In general, the maximum deductible annual contribution that can be made to the plan on behalf of an owner-employee to a defined contribution plan is the lesser of $30,000 or 25 percent of earned income (20 percent of gross self-employment income). In the case of a profit sharing plan, the percentage is 13.04 percent. Earned income is defined as income generated through the performance of personal services and does not include income produced by capital such as interest and dividend income.

Self-employed retirement plans do have some potential disadvantages. Each full-time employee with two years or more of service must be included in the plan. A full-time employee is one who works at least 1,000 hours during a given year. The employee's interest in the contribution must vest immediately and

---

[6] IRC Sec. 401

the contributions made cannot discriminate against lower-paid employees. Also distributions cannot be made from the plan to the owner-employee until he or she attains age 59-1/2, unless he or she is disabled or is willing to pay a ten percent penalty tax on the taxable amount withdrawn.

The Individual Retirement Account (IRA) is the most recent of the tax-qualified plans created by Congress.[7] Faculty members who are not active participants in either a qualified retirement plan, a government retirement plan, or a tax-sheltered annuity may establish an IRA. Further, if adjusted gross income (AGI) is less than $25,000 ($40,000 for married couples filing jointly), a faculty member may make deductible contributions to an IRA even if covered by another retirement plan. The deductible amount is reduced proportionately as AGI increases within the $10,000 phase-out range. The annual deduction for amounts contributed to an IRA is the lesser of $2,000 or 100 percent of the taxpayer's earned income or compensation. The $2,000 limitation may be raised to $2,250 if contributions are made on behalf of both the worker and the non-working spouse.

Many faculty members are already active participants in a qualified retirement plan and have AGIs beyond the permissable range and, therefore, cannot contribute to an IRA. Those faculty who can create an IRA are referred to Internal Revenue Code Section 408 for more details. Those individuals also should contact several of the banks, savings and loan associations, or insurance companies who handle Individual Retirement Accounts.

Deferred Compensation: Professor Employed by State and Local Governments

Professors employed by state and local governments may defer receiving a portion of their salaries until they retire. Under I.R.C. Sec. 457, such amounts, and the earnings thereon, will not be taxed until actually received by the employee. The maximum annual deferral is the lesser of one-third of the professor's includible compensation (net of the deferred amount), or $7,500. One-third of includible compensation is equivalent to 25 percent of a FM's gross compensation. For example, if FM's annual salary is $25,000, FM can defer a maximum of $6,250 for the taxable year ($25,000-6,250 x 1/3). Therefore, the $7,500 limitation becomes a consideration when FM's gross compensation exceeds $30,000. Amounts contributed by the employer to a tax-sheltered annuity

---

[7] IRC Sec. 408

are deducted from includible compensation. These amounts can only be received upon retirement, separation from service, death, or because of an unforseeable emergency.

Partial Withdrawal of Investment

If, before receiving any monthly benefits, a retiring faculty member first receives a large distribution of a portion of the funds accumulated in the retirement plan, this amount may be treated first as a recovery of his cost and then, as ordinary income. To qualify for this special treatment FM must have participated in the plan as of May 5, 1986 and the plan had to permit the withdrawal of FM's contributions before the annuity starting date. For example, suppose that FM should choose to receive, and his employer and the annuity company would permit, a lump-sum distribution of $3,000 to accommodate his adjustment to retirement. That $3,000 would be treated as a recovery of cost since FM's personal investment in the annuity was $14,000. Because of the withdrawal, the remaining "investment" would be decreased from $14,000 to $11,000. This would reduce the numerator of the exclusion ratio from 14 to 11. The denominator also would change since the withdrawal reduced the total fund available for distribution.

Such an early withdrawal as described in the preceding paragraph also might be received from an IRA, Keogh plan, or tax-sheltered annuity. Typically, however, the faculty member would have few, if any after-tax dollars invested in these types of plans.

Lump-Sum Distributions

The discussion above pertained to a partial lump-sum withdrawal of some of the proceeds from the retirement plan. Instead of withdrawing only part of the funds available, the taxpayer may elect to take the total amount of funds which have accumulated to his or her credit in a qualified retirement plan. A lump-sum distribution from a tax-sheltered annuity received by a faculty member less any tax basis is taxed as ordinary income in the year of receipt.[8] However, special treatment may be available for distributions from Keogh plans. If the entire balance is paid within a single year; the employee has been a participant in the plan for at least five years; and the employee

---

[8] IRC Sec. 72(e)(5)

has either (1) attained age 59-1/2, (2) died, (3) been separated from service, or (4) been disabled, the gain arising from the distribution can probably be taxed under a very favorable set of tax provisions. The most favorable treatment occurs if FM was at least age fifty on January 1, 1986.

FM Age 50 on January 1, 1986. The basic tax treatment for such "lump-sum distributions" is to tax the part of the distribution attributable to pre-1974 years of employment as capital gains (20 percent rate). The balance is treated as ordinary income. The ordinary income portion may be taxed under a procedure termed ten-year forward averaging, based upon 1986 tax rates.[9] Although this procedure is elective, it offers such favorable tax treatment, that few if any faculty would not elect to use it. Under ten-year forward averaging the portion of the gain which is to be taxed as ordinary income can be spread over a hypothetical ten-year period.

A taxpayer may elect to have the entire distribution taxed as ordinary income eligible for ten-year forward averaging. This permits the entire distribution to be spread over the hypothetical ten-year period, thereby reducing the tax paid by many taxpayers. Also, FM may elect to use a five-year forward averaging technique (to be discussed subsequently). An averaging technique can be used only once, however.

Two examples will illustrate these provisions for a FM who was at least age 50 on January 1, 1986. The first example computes the tax for a lump-sum distribution which is taxed as part capital gain and part ordinary income. To compute the tax, the faculty member must first subtract from the distribution the amount she contributed to the plan with her after-tax dollars, i.e., contributions which were not tax-sheltered. Then, she must divide the remainder (termed the taxable distribution) into two parts. The first part is that portion of the distribution which is attributable to years of plan participation before 1974. This amount is taxed as long-term capital gain. The remaining portion of the distribution relates to years of participation after 1973 and is taxed as ordinary income. It is the ordinary income portion of the distribution which is eligible for ten-year forward averaging.

The allocation of the distribution into the capital gain and ordinary income components is accomplished by multiplying the total taxable distribution by the ratio of pre-1974 participation

---

[9] IRC Sec. 402(e)

to post-1973 participation. For example, if the faculty member received a taxable lump-sum distribution of $84,000 in 1987, and was a participant in the plan from January 1, 1970 to January 1, 1977, the allocation is accomplished as follows:

$$\$84{,}000 \times \frac{48\ (1/1/70 - 12/31/73)}{84\ (1/1/70 - 1/1/77)} = \$48{,}000 \text{ taxable as capital gains}$$

$$\$84{,}000 \times \frac{36\ (1/1/74 - 1/1/77)}{84\ (1/1/70 - 1/1/77)} = \$36{,}000 \text{ taxable as ordinary income, but eligible for ten-year forward averaging}$$

The $48,000 would be included in the faculty member's tax return as a long-term capital gain and taxed at 20 percent ($9,600 taxes).

The $36,000 would be taxed under the ten-year forward averaging rules as follows (using 1986 rates and ZBA):

(1) Total taxable distribution $84,000

(2) Minimum distribution allowance (this is a
    special exclusion equal to 50 percent of
    the first $20,000 of the total distribution.
    If the distribution exceeds $20,000, the
    exclusion is reduced by 20 percent of the
    distribution in excess of $20,000. No
    minimum distribution allowance exists for a
    taxable distribution greater than $70,000).   -0-

(3) Net taxable distribution $84,000

(4) Ten percent of amount in step (3) plus $2,480
    (The $2,480 is the zero bracket amount for
    an unmarried taxpayer. It is necessary to
    add this amount for distribution made in
    in 1986 or later). $10,880

(5) Tax on amount in step (4) using the tax
    rate schedule X for 1986 $ 1,175

(6) Multiply tax computed in step (5) by 10 $11,750

(7) Percentage of ordinary income portion
    to total taxable amount ($36,000/$84,000)   42.86%

(8) Tax on ordinary income portion of
    distribution (42.86% x $11,750) $ 5,036

As a result of the distribution, the faculty member will owe taxes of $14,636 ($9,600 + $5,036) unless the election is made to have the entire distribution taxed under the ten-year forward averaging provisions. That computation would be as follows:

(1) Total taxable distribution $84,000

(2) Minimum distribution allowance   -0-

(3) Net taxable distribution $84,000

(4) Ten percent of amount in step (3) plus $2,480 $10,880

(5) Tax on amount in step (4) using the tax rate
    schedule X $ 1,175

(6) Multiply tax computed in step (5) by 10.
    This is the total tax to be paid by this
    faculty member $11,175

The faculty member would save $3,461 ($14,636 - $11,175) by electing to tax the entire distribution under ten-year forward averaging. Calculations should be made in each specific situation to determine which alternative produces the most favorable tax results.

Ten-year forward averaging is available for lump-sum distributions from qualified pension, profit sharing, stock bonus, and Keogh plans. It is not available for lump-sum distributions from an IRA or a Section 457 plan.

Ten-year forward averaging is available not only to the faculty member but also to a single (not joint) beneficiary of the plan who obtains the lump-sum distribution because of the faculty member's death. However, if the beneficiary receives a lump-sum distribution, the amount distributed cannot be excluded from the decedent's gross estate for purposes of computing the estate tax.

FM Not Age 50 on January 1, 1986. If a faculty member was not age 50 by January 1, 1986, less favorable lump-sum distribution treatment occurs. First, a one-time, five-year averaging must be used rather than ten-year averaging. Second, capital gain treatment is phased-out from 1987 until 1992 as follows:

Year	Capital Gain Portion
1987	100%
1988	95%
1989	75%
1990	50%
1991	25%
1992 and thereafter	None

A faculty member will pay the same rate on capital gain as on ordinary income. Further, the tax rates and standard deduction in the year of distribution are used for the calculations.

Rollovers of Lump-Sum Distributions[10]

Individual retirement accounts (IRAs) were discussed in an earlier section. Recall that this type of qualified retirement plan is available to those employees who are not active participants in another qualified plan or under a certain AGI maximum. In addition, IRAs serve another very important function by providing a means for "rolling over" distributions from qualified plans.

The general concept of a rollover is relatively easy to understand. It means that the employee has received a lump-sum distribution (as defined in Section 402(e)(4) from a qualified pension or annuity plan and has recontributed the amount of the lump-sum, less his or her own contributions, to an IRA. If done properly, the rollover is tax-free.

Numerous procedural rules must be satisfied if the rollover is to be successful. The lump-sum distribution must consist of the balance to the credit of the employee and must be made within one taxable year. In addition, the distribution must have been made because of:

(1) The employee's death, or
(2) The employee having attained age 59-1/2, or
(3) The employee's separation from service, or
(4) The employee having become disabled

The rollover must occur within 60 days after the lump-sum distribution is received by the employee. Therefore, the employee should try to decide if he or she wants to rollover the

---

[10] IRC Secs. 403(a)(4), 408(d)(3), and 402(a)(5)

lump-sum distribution in advance of receiving it. A drawback of a rollover is that any future lump-sum distribution from the IRA will not be eligible for ten-year or five-year forward averaging. This hold true even if the original lump-sum distribution would have been eligible, had it not been rolled-over into the IRA. A partial roll-over of at least 50 percent of the balance may be subject to tax-free treatment.

Other procedural rules may need to be satisfied by certain employees in special circumstances. The advice of a competent professional should be sought by any employee attempting a rollover.

After 1986 a faculty member covered by a Section 457 plan may elect to transfer (roll-over) any portion to another eligible deferred compensation plan without incurring a tax.

Other Types of Retirement Income

An annuity contract purchased from a mutual company may pay dividends to the retiree which are subject to the federal income tax. (Recall that the $100/$200 dividend exclusion has been repealed.)

As mentioned earlier, Social Security benefits normally will be available to the retired faculty member. Up to one-half of these benefits may be taxable.

Retirees who have accumulated other assets besides retirement benefits may utilize these assets to generate retirement income such as interest. Since the retiree will be a cash basis taxpayer, interest is taxable when actually or constructively received. If the taxpayer owns Series E or EE bonds, he or she may elect to recognize the income on an annual basis as it accrues or wait and pay taxes on the income when the bonds are redeemed.

The university or college may provide a guaranteed level of retirement benefits. If the annuity benefits are not as high as the guaranteed benefits, the university or college will pay supplementary benefits to make up the difference. These supplementary payments are taxable income and not part of the annuity stream of benefits.

Death Benefits

Assume that an employee dies and by reason of his or her death the employer makes a payment to the estate or beneficiary of the employee. If the commitment for such a payment has the elements of a life insurance contract, with the attendant risks and actuarial soundness of life insurance, the payment will be excluded from the recipient's gross income. For this reason, benefit payments under the State of Georgia Survivor's Benefit Program have been held to be life insurance payments.[11] A subsequent line of cases indicates that if another program provided benefits similar to the Georgia program, a court would determine that distributions from those programs would also be treated like life insurance.[12]

It should be recognized that most payments made by an employer to the estate or beneficiaries of a deceased employee will not be considered to be life insurance. However, some or all of these payments may still be excluded from the recipient's gross income. Under Section 101 of the Internal Revenue Code, the first $5,000 of such payments are excludable if the payments are made solely because of the employee's death. Only the portion of the payment which is related to the employer's contribution comes within this $5,000 exclusion. The portion which is a return of the employee's investment is not taxable in any event.

One word of caution. If an employee has already retired and his annuity benefit payments have begun prior to his death, his beneficiary probably will not be able to take advantage of the $5,000 exclusion. Professional advice should be secured by any beneficiary who is unsure of the nature of his or her receipts.

Transfer Tax Considerations - Estate and Gift

After 1984, there is no estate tax exclusion for employer contributions to a retirement plan. Therefore, the full amount is included in the gross estate.

Assume that the facts in a Tax Court case are altered so that a gift was made instead of a transfer at death.[13] Thus, at the time when an annuity had a value of $37,000, the employee irrevocably assigned to a designated beneficiary any benefits

---

[11] Ross v. Odom, 401 F.2d 464 (5th Cir., 1968).

[12] Kess, Standley E. v. U.S., 451 F.2d 1229 (6th Cir., 1971); Evelyn P. Davis v. U.S., 323 F.Supp. 858 (DC W. Va., 1971).

[13] L.E. Johnson, Est., 56 TC 944 (1971); acq. 1973-2 CB 2.

remaining to be paid after the employee's death. The amount of the gift would not be the $37,000 but would be a present value amount determined from the life expectancy of the employee and the provisions of the annuity contract.

The Internal Revenue Code permits a portion of this gift to be excluded from the transfer tax provisions.[14] The exclusion is similar to the exclusion of part of the annuity from the decedent's taxable estate before 1985. Thus, the portion of the gift which is attributable to the employer's contribution would not be subject to the transfer tax. This exclusion should apply to the same type of qualified retirement plans that are given similar treatment under the estate provisions before 1985. The Tax Court's reasoning in the 1971 case appears to be broad enough to apply to annuities gifted by employees of state colleges and universities.

---

[14] IRC Sec. 2517

APPENDIX TO CHAPTER II

Some Features of the Retirement System Available Through Teachers Insurance and Annuity Association and College Retirement Equities Fund (TIAA and CREF):

TIAA and CREF are available through colleges, universities, independent schools, and other non-profit and tax exempt educational and scientific institutions.

Premiums, paid individually or through an eligible institution, purchase annuity contracts provided through TIAA and CREF.

TIAA annuities guarantee a definite amount of future retirement income; CREF contracts are variable annuities.

TIAA invests almost exclusively in fixed-dollar obligations (diversified bonds and mortgages); CREF invests in common stocks.

A faculty member may have his or her premiums applied to TIAA or to CREF, or to combinations of both, subject to any restrictions placed on the allocation by the employing institution.

Premium payments may be borne entirely by the employer, entirely by the employee, or by both, depending on the employing institution.

An employee may enter these systems immediately upon being on the payroll of a participating institution, or after some delay, depending on either his or her own choice, the employer's, or both.

Benefit options which are available in TIAA and CREF include single life annuities, lifetime annuities with 10- or 20-year guarantee; survivor annuities (2/3 benefit to survivor with 10- or 20-year guarantee; or 1/2 benefit to second annuitant with 10- or 20-year guarantee); and, available through TIAA, installment refund annuities (lifetime annuities with guarantee of paying full annuity accumulation).

Upon the death of an employee who has not started receiving annuity benefits, the beneficiary may take the value in a lump-sum or in installments, unless the employee had committed the benefit payments to a specified pattern.

TIAA and CREF are fully funded, as compared with some retirement plans which are the obligation of the employer but are not fully funded.

TIAA and CREF annuity contracts are fully portable; an employee who leaves a participating institution retains ownership in the annuity contracts, including accumulations attributable to both employer and employee contributions.

The benefit payments received by TIAA annuitants will include, in addition to the guaranteed benefits, any dividends declared by TIAA.

TIAA and CREF annuity contracts do not provide for loans and do not have a cash surrender value.

The annuity payments begin at "normal retirement age" which is usually stated in the college retirement plan. This age cannot exceed 71 years.

The participating individuals may make unscheduled payments into either TIAA or CREF at any time.

Except for some situations concerning annuities that have been in force for only a short time, TIAA-CREF annuities may not be redeemed or repurchased prior to the employee's retirement or death.

TIAA and CREF permit, at the time of retirement, lump-sum distributions up to a maximum of 10 percent of the accumulations at that time; the respective employing institutions need to concur with such a plan.

TIAA and CREF permit savings plans by which individual employees may authorize their employers to deduct from monthly pay and remit as annuity contributions, savings amounts which are different from the general pattern of withholdings for retirement purposes; the respective employing institutions need to authorize these plans.

Additional annuity contributions to TIAA-CREF may be made on a tax-deferred basis under Section 403(b) of the Internal Revenue Code through a salary-reduction agreement with the employer, to the extent of the limits set by Sections 403(b) and 415 of the Internal Revenue Code.

CHAPTER III
INSURANCE PROGRAMS

Various types of insurance programs are among the most common supplemental benefits available to faculty members. Group life and accident insurance, hospital-surgical-medical coverage, major medical protection, and disability income plans are typical insurance programs. In many instances, such insurance programs are true "fringe benefits" in that the employer pays all or part of the premiums for faculty members. In other instances, the faculty member pays insurance premiums, but has the advantage of preferred "group" rates for desired coverage. Several tax benefits are available for those who have properly structured insurance programs.

At some schools, a "cafeteria" approach to insurance benefits is available. The school specifies an assortment of insurance programs and the dollar amount it will contribute for each employee; the employee can then choose the coverage he or she desires, paying individually for premiums in excess of the school's contribution. One advantage of this "cafeteria" approach is flexibility, since each employee can tailor chosen benefits to meet personal needs.

The King and Cook study, as referenced in the introduction, identified the features of common university insurance programs and their relative frequency.[1] Administrators and faculty groups responsible for university benefit programs may find a substantial amount of interesting and useful data in this 1980 study. The American Association of University Professors' (AAUP) data provided in Table 1 also may prove helpful.

Group Life Insurance

Life insurance is a useful financial planning tool for most faculty members. It can be used to replace one's earnings, provide emergency funds for heirs, and provide for liquidity and other estate planning needs. In addition, some "permanent" types of life insurance can be used as a savings program and/or a supplemental retirement income plan.

Many different types of life insurance policies are available to individuals, but such policies generally can be classified in one of two categories: term or permanent. Term insurance policies provide death benefit protection only for a specified period of time. Some term policies are renewable. Permanent policies

---

[1] King and Cook, see page 3.

provide a savings feature (cash value) as well as death benefit protection; as the cash value increases, the amount of death benefit (pure insurance) generally decreases. The savings element has investment features such as a cash surrender value, loan value, and a paid-up insurance feature; however, as compared to some investments, these non-forfeiture features are guaranteed by the insurance contract. Examples of permanent insurance include whole life (ordinary life), limited payment life (e.g., life paid-up at 65), and endowment policies.

Insurance may be purchased by or for individuals or groups of individuals. Under group coverage, participating members of the group are usually covered by the same policy. Group premium rates are generally lower than individual policy rates due to economics of scale and shared risk opportunities. Unlike individual policies, most group plans also provide protection without proof of insurability.

Most large employers, including universities, make some form of group life insurance coverage available to their employees. The employer sponsoring such coverage must decide who will pay required premiums: the employer, the employee, or both. The latter arrangement appears to be common.

Employee insurance programs have several important tax ramifications related both to premium payments and benefits paid at death. Premiums paid by the employer for group-term life insurance up to $50,000 of coverage per employee are not considered to be taxable income for the employee. If insurance in excess of $50,000 is purchased by the employer, a portion of the premium paid may be includable in the employee's income based on tables provided in the Treasury Regulations. In the unusual situation where a university purchases permanent insurance for a faculty member, the entire annual premium will likely constitute taxable income to the faculty member as additional compensation. Thus, group-term life insurance purchased by the employer provides a unique tax-sheltered fringe benefit for faculty members. Premiums paid by the faculty member are not deductible for federal income tax purposes, even when withheld from one's salary.

Generally speaking, the proceeds of life insurance policies paid at death are not subject to federal income tax. This rule applies regardless of the type of policy (group or individual, term or permanent) and beneficiary. Prior to 1987, when proceeds of life insurance were paid to a surviving spouse in installments which include interest on proceeds after the insured's death, up to $1,000 per year of interest income was excludable from the recipient's gross income. This exclusion was repealed by the Tax Reform Act of 1986.

While exempt from income tax, the proceeds of life insurance policies are normally subject to federal estate tax. In 1987, estates with a taxable value, including taxable life insurance proceeds, in excess of $600,000 may be subject to estate taxes. This estate tax consequence of life insurance can often be avoided if the individual takes one of two actions prior to death. The proceeds could be made payable to or the policy might be assigned to a qualified charitable organization. Gifts to charity generally are not subject to federal estate or gift taxes. Alternatively, a policy (or policies) could be assigned (gifted) to a family member or another individual.

To assign an insurance policy to another individual, the owner-insured must relinquish all incidents of ownership in the policy transferred. Incidents of ownership include the rights to borrow against or cash-in policies, assign ownership, and change beneficiaries. The option to assign or give away life insurance policies generally exists for both individual and group policies. However, to assign one's interest in a group policy, both the policy contract and local law must allow transfers.

One should note that gifts of life insurance policies to another individual are subject to the Federal gift tax. Gift tax laws allow a donor to give up to $10,000 per year per donee tax-free if the donee has a "present interest" (current right to enjoy) in the gift. As a result, many insurance gifts are tax-free. Gifts of a "future interest" do not qualify for the annual exclusion. For gift tax purposes, the value of a life insurance policy is its value at the date of the gift rather than the policy's face amount; term policies generally have a low gift tax value, while permanent policies have a gift tax value close to their cash surrender amount. In either case, the underwriting insurance company is obligated to provide a policyholder with a statement of the value for gift tax purposes (form 712). Federal estate tax laws require that gifts of life insurance be included in the donor's estate if the donor dies within three years of making a gift. Consequently, the proceeds of a life insurance policy will be included in the insured donor's estate if he or she dies within three years after transferring an existing insurance policy.

Administrators or faculty groups responsible for group-life insurance programs should be cognizant of the various provisions that might be included in a group policy. While program objectives and costs should control plan design, some common provisions in group policies (a) allow differential benefits based on salary brackets or salary multiples, (b) provide limited post-retirement coverage, (c) allow faculty members the option to buy additional coverage, (d) provide coverage for spouse and children (e) permit conversion to individual permanent insurance if a member leaves the institution, (f) provide a waiting period for coverage of new employees, and (g) provide accidental death and dismemberment and/or short-term disability coverage.

Medical Insurance

Another supplemental benefit available to most faculty members is medical insurance coverage. This type of benefit usually can be separated into two types of insurance, hospital-medical-surgical coverage and major medical coverage.

Hospital-medical-surgical insurance, as the name implies, provides basic coverage for common medical expenses such as hospital charges, physician's charges, medicine and drugs, and surgical costs. The scope of coverage and dollar limits vary widely from policy to policy, and faculty members and plan administrators should familiarize themselves with plan details and alternatives. Policies can be either individual or group, with group policies most common in the university setting.

Major medical insurance is also available to most faculty members. This type of plan is aimed toward major expenses, such as catastrophic illnesses, not covered under basic medical insurance. Such expenses could be items excluded under basic hospital-medical-surgical coverage or expenses in excess of basic policy dollar limits. Major medical insurance typically reimburses faculty members for approximately 80 percent of expenses beyond the basic plan payments after the employee has paid some minimal "deductible" amount. A common "deductible" amount is $100 per year.

Major medical insurance is often a separate policy from the basic coverage, but an increasing number of plans offer a combination of basic and major medical coverage. In either case, plan provisions should be coordinated to provide desired benefits at the most reasonable cost.

The various types of major medical plans available offer a wide variety of deductible features and maximum coverage limits. For example, plan limits vary from $10,000 to $250,000 or more. In some cases, such limits apply to each illness while others apply on an annually renewable or lifetime basis. Deductibles may also apply on a per illness, annual, or other basis. Consequently, plan administrators and individual faculty members should be cognizant of plan provisions and alternatives. Plan design should be determined by plan objectives and costs, and individual faculty members should attempt to have coverage consistent with personal needs and desires. If group coverage available to a faculty member is not sufficient, additional personal coverage should be considered. With recent and expected future increases in medical costs, policies with large major medical limits may be desirable.

The advent of Medicare reduced the need for medical insurance coverage beyond retirement. However, modified coverage which includes items which are not paid by Medicare and Medicaid should be considered beyond retirement. Such coverage is available to faculty members at some institutions through the university sponsored plan; in other instances, personal supplemental coverage may be desired or required.

There are several tax implications of medical insurance and medical expenses. As with group-term life insurance, the tax advantages of medical insurance coverage are clearly with employer-financed plans. Premiums paid by the employer do not result in taxable income for the faculty member, and benefit payments (to the extent of medical expenses) are tax-free, even when the spouse and dependents are included in the plan. If the faculty member pays part or all of medical insurance premiums, benefits are still tax-free, and premium payments are deductible within specified limits (discussed below). One should note that plans under which premium costs are shared by the university and faculty members have the advantage of allowing a standard contribution by the employer for all faculty members, while providing the flexibility of variable coverage where individual needs may be quite different.

Medical expenses can be deducted by individual taxpayers if they elect to "itemize" deductions rather than claiming the standard deduction. Under current law, medical expenses, including insurance premiums, generally can be deducted to the extent they exceed 7.5% of an individual's adjusted gross income. Of course, medical expenses paid or reimbursed by the insurance company or employer may not be deducted by the individual. Thus, a well-insured taxpayer will probably find that his or her unreimbursed expenses do not exceed 7.5% of adjusted gross income, and no medical expense deduction is available.

One should note that only "medical" insurance premiums are deductible. If some medical benefits for the taxpayer and dependents are included in other policies, such as disability policies, only the medical portion is deductible. An itemized premium notice or separate statement from the insurance company is needed to substantiate the medical expense deduction. If combination coverage is provided in an employer sponsored plan, the university should provide deduction information to its faculty members.

Many professors will carry their principal family medical coverage through a university plan; however, one should investigate individual policies and group coverage available to other family members. Individual policies may be advisable to cover "gaps" in group plans. Children are often eligible for insurance at school, and a working spouse may qualify for a separate employee plan. Such plans may be easily coordinated with a university plan, and they are frequently subsidized or available at a low cost.

Disability Insurance

Many faculty members also have short and/or long-term disability benefits available to them through either university-sponsored programs or individual disability insurance policies. While the risk of disability is not normally high for college faculty members, the financial consequences of disability and the associated potential loss of income could be disastrous. Some form of disability coverage is generally desirable.

Short-term disability benefits are generally available through formal sick pay plans or informal arrangements within a faculty member's department. Partial long-term disability benefits are often available through the federal Social Security system and university retirement programs. Other disability income could be provided through personal savings or insurance policies.

There are several important tax ramifications of disability benefits. Benefits provided through the federal Social Security system are tax-free to recipients. Benefits provided through an individual policy purchased by a faculty member are also generally tax-free on receipt; however, the individual's premium payments are not tax deductible.

In the case of employer financed plans covering short-term or long-term disability, the cost (or premiums) paid by the employer generally is not included in the employee's income. One should note, however, that benefits received by a faculty member would normally be subject to tax as compensation. Under pre-1984 law, benefits paid by an employer for sickness or injuries under a qualified sick pay plan were subject to a limited exclusion from income. This sick pay exclusion was repealed, and former employees under age 65 who are totally and permanently disabled and receiving disability retirement pay now qualify for the more general retirement income credit of Code Sec. 22.

The special tax credit is based on an "initial amount," equal to the smaller of the disability income or a "base amount" of $5,000 (single), $7,500 (married filing jointly), or $3,750 (married filing separately). The initial amount is reduced by certain excludable pension benefits (e.g., social security, railroad retirement, etc.) and by one-half of taxpayer's adjusted gross income exceeding $7,500 (single), $10,000 (married filing jointly), or $5,000 (married filing separtely). The base amount as adjusted is eligible for a 15 percent credit (limited to the total tax liability).[2]

Faculty members should be aware that provisions of disability insurance policies vary substantially from policy to policy with respect to such key items as definitions of disability, waiting period for benefits, covered sickness or injury, duration of benefits, and amount of benefits. One should be sure that options and provisions selected are consistent with personal needs, desires, and other available coverage.

In summary, life insurance, medical insurance, and disability insurance programs offer security and economic benefits as well as possible tax benefits to faculty members. Employer-financed group-term life insurance programs and medical insurance programs offer special tax advantages, since both premium payments and benefits received are generally excludable from the faculty member's gross income.

---

[2] IRC Sec. 22

CHAPTER IV
SCHOLARSHIPS, FELLOWSHIPS, AND AWARDS

Scholarships and Fellowships

The Tax Reform Act of 1986 (TRA) made some dramatic changes in the income tax treatment of scholarships and fellowships.[1] Many receipts that formerly were excluded from income are now taxable--they no longer receive such preferential treatment. Nonetheless, even though greater restrictions apply, some scholarships and fellowships may still totally or partially escape income taxation. For example, under the old law, except for certain limitations, any amount properly characterized as a scholarship or fellowship awarded to a degree candidate was excludable from income. Under current law, however, only the portion of the scholarship or fellowship grant which actually goes for tuition, and course-required fees, books, supplies, or equipment is excludable from income, and only if the amount is received by a degree candidate. Any other amounts, earmarked for expenditures such as room, board or incidental expenses, are includible in the income of the recipient. Further, amounts received in excess of the cost of tuition, books, and so forth are not excludable from income. The new rules apply to taxable years beginning after December 31, 1986, but only in the case of scholarships and fellowships granted after August 16, 1986.

In the Treasury Regulations, a scholarship is defined as "an amount paid or allowed to, or for the benefit of, a student, whether an undergraduate or a graduate, to aid such individual in pursuing his studies." An educational institution is defined as one "which normally maintains a regular faculty and curriculum and normally has a regularly organized body of students in attendance at the place where its educational activities are carried on."

Those same Regulations define a fellowship as a grant to be received by or expended for the benefit of an individual "to aid him in the pursuit of his study or research."[2] Note that no mention is made of an educational institution in connection with study or research for the fellowship grant. For example, an award granted by the National Foundation on the Arts and Humanities to a writer engaged in writing a novel and in the continuation of his poetic work was treated as a non-taxable

---

[1] IRC Sec. 117

[2] Regs. Sec. 1.117-3(a)-(c)

fellowship.[3] However, under post-1986 law, the receipt would be taxable unless the research fellow is a candidate for a degree.

The Supreme Court has upheld the validity of the definitions contained in the Regulations, stating that the definitions comport with "the ordinary understanding of 'scholarships' and 'fellowships' as relatively disinterested, 'no strings' educational grants, with no requirement of any substantial quid pro quo from the recipients."[4] Thus, the primary distinction between a scholarship or fellowship grant and compensation depends on whether the primary purpose for making the grant is to enable the recipient to further his education or training in his individual capacity or to compensate him for past, present or future services.

In contrast to prior law, the terms "scholarship" or "fellowship" would not include services and accommodations (room, board, laundry services, etc.), but they could include the amount of tuition, matriculation, and other fees which are furnished or remitted to aid the recipient in the pursuit of study or research. Furthermore, payments in the nature of a family allowance would not be considered part of a scholarship or fellowship grant.

No amounts may be excluded as a scholarship or fellowship if provided by a relative, friend, or one motivated by family considerations. Of course, these amounts may be non-taxable gifts.

One who is a candidate for a degree is treated more favorably with respect to scholarships and fellowships under post-1986 laws than one who is not a degree candidate. There is no dollar limitation on amounts that may be excluded by a degree candidate either for a scholarship or for a fellowship. Under pre-1987 law, non-degree-seeking recipients were limited to an exclusion of $300 per month, and only grants from certain types of grantors were excluded. However, the TRA repeals the exclusion for non-degree candidates entirely, beginning for years after December 31, 1986, but only for those scholarships and fellowships granted after August 16, 1986.

Regardless of one's status as a candidate for a degree, any amount received as payment for part-time employment may not be excluded. Thus, one who receives a scholarship or fellowship but

---

[3] Revenue Ruling 72-163, 1972-1 CB 26

[4] Bingler v. Johnson, 394 U.S. 741 (1969)

is required to teach, conduct research or perform any other services must include in income an amount equal to the rate of compensation ordinarily paid for similar services if performed by an individual who is not the recipient of a scholarship or a fellowship grant.

Under pre-TRA law, an amount could be excluded from income by degree candidates if teaching, research, or other services was required of all such candidates and the primary purpose of the grant was to benefit the recipient rather than the institution.[5] However, this opportunity generally is no longer available for amounts received after December 31, 1986. Therefore, such amounts received for services rendered, even if they are required of all candidates in a degree program, are to be included in the income of the recipient. No exclusion is permitted for any portion of the grant which is conditioned on the performance of past, present, or future services.

Under prior law, a scholarship or fellowship recipient could exclude from gross income amounts specifically designated to cover travel expenses, research, clerical help or equipment if such expenses are incident to a scholarship or fellowship grant which is excludable from income. Further, the payments received were to have been actually spent for those expenses during the term of the scholarship or fellowship grant and within a reasonable time before and after such term. However, under the portion of the current law that covers scholarships and fellowships, there is no provision (as there was under prior law) for exclusion of such amounts that are to be used to cover certain research-related expenses and equipment. But rather, the appropriate treatment would be to include such amounts in the income of the taxpayer, and then, to the extent possible under other provisions of the law, claim deductions from that income (e.g., as an employee business expense--see CHAPTER VI, PROFESSIONAL EXPENSES AND REIMBURSEMENTS).

Grants to Faculty

Many institutions encourage members of the faculty to perform research by providing funds for research support. Obviously, if the grants are not taxable, an institution may be able to utilize fewer resources to stimulate more research activity than would be the case if the grants are deemed taxable. As was the case under prior law, there is not a provision, even

---

[5] See Revenue Ruling 75-280, 1975-2 CB 47, which summarizes the conditions that must apply in order for the exclusion to apply under prior law.

for partial exclusion, received by faculty who are not degree candidates. Thus, the current law treats all such receipts as compensation for services rendered to or on behalf of the grantor and as a result, fully taxable.

If a faculty member is involved in a long-term sponsored research project for which the funding was granted prior to August 17, 1986, the taxpayer would be able to utilize pre-TRA law and exclude as much as $300 per month for up to 36 months even if the amounts are received after December 31, 1986.[6] However, for those research grants awarded after August 16, 1986, the amounts received after December 31, 1986 are subject to taxation by the non-degree candidate faculty recipient. Unfortunately, a faculty member is not likely to be a candidate for a degree. Offsetting deductions, however, are available (subject to certain limits) for costs that qualify as business expenses.

Under prior law, because of the numerous factors which had to be considered when attempting to ascertain whether a grant was a scholarship or fellowship, taxpayers were frequently confronted with a situation where the appropriate tax treatment was not clear. Under the current law, taxpayers should not be confronted with as much uncertainty as under pre-TRA law. Unfortunately, the price that taxpayers pay for the reduction in uncertainty is having many more receipts subject to tax than was the case earlier. Because many students rely on scholarships and fellowships to make higher education affordable, the new tax provisions have generally made education more expensive.

Tax-Free Scholarships and Fellowships - Undesirable Consequences

Throughout this section, it has been assumed that taxpayers would prefer to have a grant treated as a non-taxable scholarship or fellowship as opposed to gross income. A taxpayer may prefer that a scholarship or fellowship be treated as taxable compensation since the payment would be treated as earned income and thus enable the taxpayer to receive the earned income credit. The earned income credit is a refundable credit available to certain low income taxpayers. The Tax Reform Act of 1986

---

[6] For additional reading in this area regarding the appropriate treatment under prior law, see Outslay and Weber, "Minimizing the Tax Cost of Faculty Research Grants," The Journal of the American Taxation Association, Spring 1986; Raabe and Willis, "Requirements for Exclusion of Fellowship Grants," Taxes, March 1977; Dilley and Wheatley, "Tax Considerations in Research Grants to Faculty," The Accounting Review, October 1977.

increased the maximum amount of allowable earned income credit to $800 from $550. The credit is equal to 14 percent of the first $5,714 of earned income received less 10 percent of excess of earned income, or adjusted gross income, whichever is higher, over $6500 in 1987, and $9000 in 1988 and later years. Because the benefit of the earned income credit is phased out as one's income increases, a taxpayer in 1987 would not receive any benefit once income exceeds $14,500 and in 1988, $17,000. The maximum credit and the phase-out income levels are to be adjusted for inflation in later years. Earned income includes wages, salaries, tips, other employee compensation and net earnings from self-employment. Further, in order to qualify, a wage earner must maintain a household that is the primary residence of the worker and a child, and the child must qualify as a dependent.[7]

Prizes and Awards

Generally, prizes and awards, except scholarships and fellowships as previously discussed, are included in the recipient's gross income. As is the case with many other types of income, the tax treatment of certain types of prizes and awards has changed, effective for prizes and awards granted after December 31, 1986.[8] Under prior law, any amount received as a prize or award was excluded if (1) it was made primarily in recognition of past achievement for religious, charitable, scientific, educational, artistic, literary or civic accomplishments; (2) the recipient was selected without any action on his part; and (3) the recipient was not required to render substantial future services as a condition to receiving the prize or award.[9]

After 1986, the exclusion for certain prizes and awards for charitable, scientific, artistic, and similar achievements is to apply only if the winner assigns the prize or award to a tax-exempt charity. Further, no charitable contribution deduction is available; otherwise a double benefit would arise from both the exclusion and deduction.

An additional limited exception to the general rule is available where certain employee prizes and awards for length of service or safety achievement are granted. All other prizes or awards from employers to employees are included in income of the

---

[7] IRC Sec. 32

[8] IRC Sec. 74

[9] IRC Sec 74(a) & (b)

taxpayer except for de minimis fringe benefits excludable under another section of the law.[10] (See CHAPTER VII, OTHER FRINGE BENEFITS.)

Possibly an award which would not qualify as a non-taxable award may be treated as an excludable scholarship or fellowship. Awards made by an exempt foundation to stimulate higher scholastic achievement among students majoring in accounting and to encourage students to specialize in the field are not excludable as prizes and awards but are excludable as scholarships.[11] A prize awarded by a business firm as part of an advertising campaign was excluded since the prize was a scholarship to be used by the winner only when enrolled as a candidate for a college degree.[12] However, a scholarship given as a prize is included in gross income if the recipient is not required to use it for educational purposes.[13]

When goods or services are provided as a taxable prize or award, the fair market value of those goods and services is included in gross income. Although the facts of each case must be considered when attempting to determine fair market value, the Tax Court has ruled that the fair market value for marketable goods is resale value less selling expenses.[14] If the goods or services are not marketable, the price which the recipient would normally be willing to pay is included in gross income.[15]

---

[10] See IRC Sec. 132(c)

[11] Revenue Ruling 66-241, 1966-2 CB 40

[12] Revenue Ruling 59-80, 1959-1 CB 39

[13] Revenue Ruling 65-58, 1965-1 CB 37

[14] L.W. McCoy, 38 TC 841 (1962)

[15] Reginald Turner, 13 TCM 462 (1954)

CHAPTER V

TAX CONSEQUENCES OF RELOCATION

College professors tend to be a mobile group, and job changes are frequent. When such a change does occur, important income tax provisions should be considered by both the employer and employee. This section proposes to address some of the more important of these provisions applicable to an individual making a permanent move as well as to one serving as a visiting professor. Major topics to be discussed include employment-seeking expenses, moving expenses, sale of a personal residence and tax factors which should be considered by a visiting professor.

Employment-Seeking Expenses

Tax rules concerning seeking and securing employment are the same for professors interested in either permanent or visiting positions. First, it is well established that reimbursements to the prospective faculty member for the cost of transportation, meals, lodging, and other similar costs do not constitute income to the professor to the extent that they do not exceed expenses actually incurred.[1] If the spouse is also included in the interview trip at the insistence or request of the prospective employing school, reimbursement of those expenses should not produce income.

Employment agency fees and other expenses incurred for the purpose of seeking employment in the same trade or business are deductible regardless of whether employment is obtained. However, such expenses related to securing a position in a new trade or business are not deductible.[2] Because a person entering the labor market for the first time is not engaged in a trade or business at the time the expenses are incurred, employment-seeking expenses are not deductible.

Since the term "trade or business" as it relates to employment-seeking fees has not been fully developed, controversy may arise in this area. If employment-seeking expenses are incurred to obtain employment with similar duties and responsibilities, the deduction should be allowed. However, if

---

[1] Revenue Ruling 63-77, 1963-1 CB 177

[2] Revenue Ruling 77-16, 1977-1 CB 37; Leonard J. Cremona, 58 TC 219 (1970), acq., 1975-1 CB 1; David J. Primuth, 54 TC 374 (1970)

the new employment involves significantly different duties and responsibilities, the IRS may argue that such expenses were incurred to enter a new trade or business and thus are not deductible.

A problem may occur when an employee who has not been active in his trade or business for an extended period of time incurs employment-seeking expenses to secure a job in that trade or business. Possibly, the lack of continuous employment may cause the deduction to be disallowed. However, one court held that a teacher who attended graduate school for 12 months was still in the same trade or business as long as she intended to resume her teaching activities at some future date.[3]

Deductible employment-seeking expenses include the cost of travel if the trip is made primarily for business purposes. If the trip is not primarily for business, the cost of the trip is not deductible, but expenses incurred during the visit which relate to seeking new employment in the same trade or business may be deducted. After December 31, 1986, travel and transportation expenses incurred when seeking employment in the same trade or business as well as other expenses such as typing, printing, and mailing a resume are treated as itemized deductions unless they are reimbursed and the reimbursement is included in gross income.[4] In addition, under the 1986 Act only 80 percent of the cost of meals is deductible and the total of such expenses is deductible only to the extent it exceeds 2 percent of the taxpayer's adjusted gross income.

Since there may be doubt as to the deductibility of one's employment-seeking expenses, reimbursement of interview and other related expenses, which does not produce gross income, may be viewed as an important benefit for professors. If there is a choice between reimbursing an equivalent dollar amount of moving expenses, which are deductible in any event, or employment-seeking expenses, which may not be deductible, probably the latter should be reimbursed.

Moving Expenses

Once a professor has secured a new permanent position, the deduction for moving expenses as well as the tax treatment of any reimbursement must be considered. In order to obtain a moving

---

[3] M. O. Furner, 393 F.2d 292 (7th Cir., 1968)

[4] IRC Sec 62(a)(2)

expenses deduction, the move must be connected with the commencement of work at a new principal place of work. Although it is not necessary for one to have made arrangements to work prior to moving to a new location, no deduction is allowed unless employment or self-employment does occur.

For an employee, the term "commencement of work" includes the beginning of work for either (a) the first time or after a substantial period of unemployment or part-time employment, (b) a different employer, or (c) the same employer. For a self-employed individual, work at the new location may be related to either the same or a new trade or business.[5]

The term "new principal place of work" refers to that place where the taxpayer's primary business activities are centered which is generally the place where he or she spends the greater portion of working time.[6] If a taxpayer has more than one place of work, "principal place" is determined on the basis of the particular circumstances in each case. Generally, a college professor's principal place of work would be a university, college, or research institute.

In order for the expenses to qualify as deductible moving expenses, it is necessary for the move to bear a reasonable proximity both in time and place to the commencement of work. Moving expenses incurred within one year of the date that work begins are normally considered to be reasonably proximate in time. If the moving expenses are not incurred within one year of the date the taxpayer begins his new work, the expenses will not be deductible unless it can be shown that special circumstances existed which prevented the taxpayer from incurring the moving expenses within the one-year period.[7] Reasonable proximity in place is discussed below in connection with the distance criteria.

During the 12-month period immediately following the move, the taxpayer who is an employee must be employed full-time for at least 39 weeks. If one is self-employed during the 24-month period immediately following the move, he or she must meet this 39-week rule and also must be employed full-time for at least 78 weeks of that 24-month period. Generally, the date of arrival

---

[5] IRC Sec. 217(a); Reg. Sec. 1.217-2(a)(3)

[6] Reg. Sec. 1.217-2(c)(3)

[7] Reg. Sec. 1.217-2(a)(3)

is the date of the termination of the last trip preceding the taxpayer's commencement of work on a regular basis and is not the date the taxpayer's family or household effects arrive.[8] Since the requirement does not mean 39 weeks for the same employer, but rather 39 weeks in the same general commuting area, taxpayers may change jobs during the year. Also, the "full-time" requirement depends upon the customary practices of the occupation in the geographic area in which the taxpayer works. If employment occurs on a seasonal basis, weeks occurring in the off-season may be counted as weeks of full-time employment provided the taxpayer's employment contract covers the off-season period and the taxpayer works for at least six months.[9] Therefore, a teacher whose contract covers a 12-month period, and who teaches on a full-time basis for at least six months, would be considered a full-time employee for the entire 12-month period. A taxpayer is treated as performing services on a full-time basis during any week of involuntary absence due to events beyond one's control such as physical illness, injury, strikes, and natural disasters. Finally, the work period requirement is waived if the taxpayer dies or employment is involuntarily terminated, other than for willful misconduct.[10] Where both husband and wife work, weeks worked by one spouse may not be added to those worked by the other in determining whether the 39-week test has been satisfied. Thus, to qualify for the deduction, the test must be met independently by at least one spouse.

In many cases, the taxpayer may not have satisfied the 39-week test when it is time to prepare the return for the year in which the move occurred. Despite this fact, a moving expense deduction may be claimed. If the deduction is not claimed and the test is subsequently satisfied, an amended return or a claim for refund may be filed. If a deduction is claimed but the taxpayer then fails to meet the 39-week or 78-week tests, an amount equal to the deduction must be included in income for the year in which it is determined that the taxpayer is no longer able to satisfy the minimum period of employment test.[11]

To qualify for the deduction, a distance test must be

---

[8] IRC Sec. 217(c)(2); Reg. Sec. 1.217-2(c)(4)

[9] Regs. Sec. 1.217-2(c)(4)(iii)&(iv)

[10] IRC Sec. 217(d)(1); Reg. Sec. 1.217-2(d)(1)

[11] IRC Sec. 217(c)(1); Reg. Sec. 1.217-2(c)(2)

satisfied.[12] For purposes of applying the minimum distance condition, all taxpayers are divided into one of two categories: taxpayers having a former principal place of work and taxpayers who are seeking full-time employment either for the first time (such as recent college graduates) or after a substantial period of unemployment. In the case of a taxpayer having a former principal place of work, no deduction is allowable unless the distance between the former residence and the new principal place of work exceeds by at least 35 miles the distance between the former residence and the former principal place of work. For a taxpayer not having a former principal place of work, no deduction is allowable unless the distance between the former residence and the new principal place of work is at least 35 miles. In applying the distance criteria, the distance between two geographic points is measured by the shortest of the more commonly traveled routes between such points.

As mentioned earlier, the move must bear a reasonably close proximity in place to commencement of duties at the new place of work. In general, a move is not considered to be reasonably proximate in place when the distance between the taxpayer's new residence and new principal place of work exceeds the distance between the former residence and the new principal place of work unless one is required, as a condition of employment, to reside at the new residence, or if such residency results in an actual decrease in commuting time or expense.[13] Note that it is possible to meet the 35-mile distance test and still not qualify for the deduction because the move does not comply with the "reasonable proximity in place" test. For example, assume a professor changes to another school located in the same metropolitan area as the former employer and the distance between the former residence and new principal place of work is 50 miles, whereas the distance between the former residence and the former principal place of work is 13 miles. Thus, the minimum distance test is satisfied. However, if the professor's new residence is more than 50 miles from the new principal place of work, the "reasonable proximity in place" test is not met.

Deductible moving expenses[14] include reasonable expenses of travel for the taxpayer and members of the household from the taxpayer's old residence to the new place of residence. The cost

---

[12] IRC Sec. 217(c)(1); Reg. Sec. 1.217-2(c)(2)

[13] Reg. Sec. 1.217-2(a)(3)

[14] IRC Sec. 217(b); Reg. Sec. 1.217-2(b)

associated with traveling the most direct route available by conventional means of transportation in as much time as is commonly required in light of the distance, travel conditions, and mode of transportation is normally used as the standard for a reasonable amount. If an automobile is used as transportation when moving, the taxpayer may deduct either the actual out-of-pocket expenses incurred, or a standard mileage rate of nine cents per mile plus parking fees and tolls.[15] Depreciation on the automobile is not included as a moving expense.[16]

In addition to transportation expenses, travel expenses also include expenses for meals and lodging incurred while in route, on the day of arrival, and possibly in the general location of the former residence if incurred within one day after the former residence is no longer suitable for occupancy. To be considered reasonable, expenditures for meals and lodging must not be lavish or extravagant.

It is not necessary for all members of the household to travel together or at the same time. Neither a tenant residing in the taxpayer's residence nor an individual such as a servant, governess, chauffeur, nurse, valet or personal attendant is considered to be a member of the taxpayer's household.

The term "old residence" refers to the taxpayer's principal residence before his or her departure to a new place of work. The term "new place of residence" refers to the taxpayer's principal residence within the area of the taxpayer's new principal place of work. Neither term includes seasonal residences, such as a summer beach cottage, or other residences used or maintained by the taxpayer or by members of the family.

Reasonable expenses of transporting household goods and personal effects of the taxpayer and members of the household, as well as the expenses of connecting or disconnecting utilities, packing, crating, intransit storage and insurance for such goods and effects are deductible. The expenses of moving these items to a taxpayer's new residence from a place other than the former residence are allowable, but only to the extent that such expenses are not in excess of the amount which would have been allowable had the move been from the taxpayer's former residence. However, expenses of transporting household goods and personal

---

[15] Revenue Procedure 82-61, 1982-2 CB 849 as modified by Revenue Procedure 85-49, 1985-2 CB 716

[16] Revenue Ruling 70-656, 1970-2 CB 67

effects purchased while en route from the taxpayer's former residence to the new residence are not deductible. Household pets[17] are considered to be household goods and personal effects.

Expenses incurred in pre-move, house-hunting trips for transportation, meals and lodging for the taxpayer and household members are deductible, subject to a limit, if the principal purpose for making the trip is to search for a new residence. Furthermore, the taxpayer must have obtained employment before incurring the pre-move expenses.

Within limits, temporary living expenses for the costs of meals and lodging are deductible if incurred by the taxpayer and members of the household while waiting in the general location of the new principal place of work to move into permanent quarters. These costs may be incurred within any period of 30 consecutive days after obtaining employment. Temporary living expenses do not include the cost of entertainment, laundry, transportation, or other personal expenses.

Moving expenses also include "qualified" expenses incident to a sale, purchase, or lease of a residence which includes a house, apartment, cooperative dwelling unit, condominium dwelling unit, or other similar dwelling. Qualified residence sale expenses are those reasonable expenses incurred incident to the sale or exchange of a former residence. Examples of sale-related expenses include commissions, escrow fees, and similar expenses reasonably necessary to dispose of the taxpayer's residence. However, "fixing-up" expenses incurred in order to assist in its sale are not considered sale-related expenses.

Qualified residence purchase expenses are those reasonable expenses incident to the purchase of a new residence in the general location of the new principal place of employment. Examples of purchase-related expenses include attorney's fees, escrow fees, appraisal fees, title costs, and "points" or loan placement charges which do not represent interest. However, payments of real estate taxes, interest and telephone installation costs are outside the scope of purchase-related expenses deductible as moving expenses.

Qualified lease expenses include reasonable expenses incident to the settlement of an unexpired lease on property used by the taxpayer as a former residence, or incident to the acquisition of a lease by the taxpayer on property to be used as

---

[17] Revenue Ruling 66-305, 1966-2 CB 102

the new residence. However, expenses incident to the settlement of an unexpired lease do not include the legal expenses of breaking an unexpired lease and expenses incident to the acquisition of a lease do not include security deposits or prepayments of rent.

The deduction for the sum of the house-hunting travel expenses plus temporary living expenses at the new place of work is limited to a maximum of $1,500. In addition, the deduction for qualified residence sale, purchase, or lease expenses is limited to $3,000 reduced by the sum of the house-hunting travel expenses and temporary living expenses at the new location.[18]

As to reporting requirements, employers are required to give employees a detailed breakdown of payments for moving expenses made after July 23, 1971. Form 4782, Employee Moving Expense Information, may be used for this purpose. This form is for information purposes only and does not have to be filed with the employee's return, however; it must be furnished to the employee by no later than January 31, following the taxable year during which the moving expenses were incurred.

All reimbursements, either direct or indirect, for the costs of moving must be included in the recipient's gross income. This inclusion normally would require income tax and Social Security withholding. However, if the employer can reasonably conclude that an equivalent moving expense deduction will be allowed, then there is no requirement for either income tax or Social Security tax withholding.[19] School administrators should be particularly aware of this treatment because of the opportunity to provide teachers with an additional bonus which will not be reduced by the Social Security tax.

Generally, moving expenses are deductible in the year paid or incurred. However, it is possible for a cash-basis taxpayer to deduct the expenses in the same year that reimbursement is received provided the expense is paid in the year prior to the year in which reimbursement is received or the expense is paid in the year immediately following the year in which reimbursement is received. In the latter case, the expense must be paid by the due date for filing the return for the year when the reimbursement was received.[20] As a result of this flexibility,

---

[18] IRC Sec. 217(b)(3)(A)

[19] IRC Sec. 3401(a)(15); Revenue Ruling 70-482, 1970-2 CB 200

[20] Reg. Sec. 1.217-2(a)(2)

taxpayers may have the opportunity to do some tax planning with respect to the deduction, especially if one has some control over the timing of the reimbursement.

After December 31, 1986, the moving expense deduction will be allowed only if the taxpayer itemizes. Of course, adequate records to substantiate the year of the move and the amounts of moving costs actually incurred should be maintained. Taxpayers may use Form 3903, Moving Expense Adjustment, for purposes of reporting this deduction.

Non-recognition of Gain on Sale of a Residence

If certain conditions described in the IRC Section 1034 are satisfied, taxpayers must defer recognition of any gain realized on the sale of a personal residence. Both the criteria that must be met in order to qualify for non-recognition and the computational procedures associated with such non-recognition will be described below.

The property disposed of must be used as the taxpayer's principal residence which generally means that the taxpayer must have occupied the property as a primary place of abode. However, the taxpayer does not have to be occupying the residence on the date of sale. Also non-recognition is available even though the residence has been temporarily rented before its sale.[21] Houseboats and house trailers may qualify as a principal residence[22] and vacant land associated with the residence has been considered as part of the residence.[23]

The taxpayer must acquire a new principal residence within a specified time period. If the new residence is purchased, it must be acquired within 24 months before or 24 months after the date of sale of the old residence. Furthermore, the taxpayer must occupy and use the new residence not later than 24 months after the old residence is sold.

This non-recognition provision will not apply with respect to the sale of a principal residence if a taxpayer has utilized the provisions of Section 1034 to defer any part of a gain on the

---

[21] R.G. Chapman, 63 TC 505 (1975); Ann K. Demeter, TC Memo 1971-209; Revenue Ruling 59-72, 1959-1 CB 203

[22] Reg. Sec. 1.1034-1(c)(3)(i)

[23] Revenue Ruling 76-541, 1976-2 CB 246

sale of a personal residence within 24 months of the current sale. However, this limitation rule does not apply when the sale is in connection with the commencement of work by the taxpayer at a new principal place of work and the residence sold is considered to be the former residence for purposes of determining the moving expense deduction. The distance and time of employment tests used for the moving expense deduction must also be satisfied.

If the criteria of Section 1034 are satisfied, the taxpayer must compare the adjusted sales price of the old residence with the cost of purchasing the new residence in order to determine the amount of realized gain, if any, which will be deferred. Realized gain is the excess of amount realized, selling price less selling expenses, over the basis of the old residence.

All of the realized gain will be deferred if the cost of the new residence exceeds the adjusted sales price of the old residence. The adjusted sales price is the amount realized less fixing-up expenses. If the adjusted sales price exceeds the cost of the new residence, part or possibly all of the realized gain must be recognized. The amount of realized gain which is recognized is equal to the excess of the adjusted sales price over the cost of the new residence, but never more than the total amount of gain realized.

Note that selling expenses are used to compute the realized gain and also to determine the gain deferred. Fixing-up expenses, however, are used only when testing to see if any of the gain must be deferred. Selling expenses include real estate commissions, advertising costs, fees for deed preparation and other expenses reasonably related to the sale. Fixing-up expenses include expenses for work performed on the old residence in order to assist in its sale. The expenses must be incurred within a 90-day period ending on the date of sale, and payment of the expenses must occur within 30 days after the sale. Fixing-up expenses do not include: allowable deductions for computing taxable income; expenses affecting the amount realized on the sale; and costs which should be capitalized as part of the basis of the old residence.

The cost of purchasing the new residence is the total of all amounts attributable to acquiring the new residence including the amounts of any mortgage or other debts to which the new residence is subject. If the new residence is acquired by an exchange of properties, the fair market value of the new residence on the date of exchange is considered to be its acquisition cost. If the taxpayer builds the replacement residence, the acquisition cost is the total of all capital expenditures associated with the construction. In addition, commissions and other such expenses are included as costs of acquiring the new residence. However, only those costs paid or incurred within the period beginning 24 months before the date of sale of the old residence and ending 24 months after the date of sale shall be considered as the cost of purchasing the new residence.

By complying with the provisions of Section 1034, the taxpayer is able to defer, not exclude, a gain on the sale of a personal residence. This deferred gain eventually may be taxed when the new residence is sold, since the adjusted basis for the new residence is equal to the cost of the new residence less the gain deferred. Of course, the taxpayer may continue to defer a gain on the sale of a personal residence by acquiring a new residence for more than the adjusted selling price of the old residence.

Exclusion of Gain on Sale of a Residence

Taxpayers who have attained age 55 may elect to exclude up to $125,000 of the gain realized on the sale of a personal residence.[24] The residence must have been the taxpayer's principal residence for at least three years of the five-year period immediately prior to the date of sale.

The $125,000 exclusion may be taken only once by a taxpayer and there is no carryover of any unused portion of the exclusion. It is possible to combine the elective provision with Section 1034, and thus a taxpayer with a gain greater than $125,000 may be able to exclude $125,000 and defer all or part of the remaining gain.

Tax Planning When Moving and Selling a Personal Residence

Expenses related to the sale of a residence may either be deducted as moving expenses or used to reduce the amount realized on the sale of a personal residence. By reducing the amount realized, both the gain realized and the adjusted selling price will be less.

Similarly, purchase-related expenses may be deducted as moving expenses or used to increase the cost of the new residence. By increasing the cost of the new residence, the taxpayer will increase the basis of the residence and may also be able to defer a greater portion of the realized gain.

---

[24] IRC Sec. 121

As a result of this alternative treatment of sale-related and purchase-related expenses, taxpayers are often faced with the question of whether to deduct them as moving expenses or either use them to reduce the amount realized or to increase the cost of the new residence. In general, taxpayers will derive greater benefit by deducting the expenses since this deduction reduces gross income. Furthermore, any recognized gain on the sale of a residence will be treated as a capital gain which can be offset with capital losses and which may someday once again be subject to preferential tax rates.

Since no more than $3,000 of sale and purchase-related expenses may be deducted as moving expenses, taxpayers may find it necessary to treat only part of such expenses as moving expenses. If the sales commission on the sale of a personal residence amounted to $4,000, the taxpayer might deduct $3,000 as a moving expense and treat $1,000 as a reduction of the selling price. When making such a decision, one must consider the fact that the $3,000 limit applies to other moving expenses such as house-hunting trips and temporary living costs at the new job location. If the taxpayer in the above example spent $400 for a house-hunting trip, only $2,600 of the sales commissions should be deducted as a moving expense.

Of course, there are situations where one may not find it advantageous to treat these sale and purchase-related expenses as moving expenses. If the costs are incurred in a year when one has a small amount of taxable income, it may be more desirable to allow the sale and purchase-related expenses to be reflected in the residence transactions.

Tax Considerations for a Visiting Professor

It is not uncommon for a professor to secure a temporary position at a new geographical location. When such an event does occur, the professor should be able to deduct travel expenses related to any trade or business which are reasonable in amount, and incurred while away from home.[25] In most cases, the deductibility of a visiting professor's travel expenses will hinge on whether he or she is, in fact, "away from home." While the questions of what constitutes a taxpayer's home has been subject to considerable litigation, it generally is considered to be the taxpayer's principal place of employment. A professor who is temporarily away from his or her principal place of employment

---

[25] IRC Sec. 162(c)(2)

should be able to maintain that he or she is away from home.[26]

The visiting professor must be prepared to provide evidence that his or her tax home has remained at the original place of employment. To accomplish this objective, the visiting professor should maintain as many connections with that location as possible. Obviously, there is no problem if there is an explicit obligation to return to the original job. If no such obligation exists, then evidence of an intent to return may include continued ownership of a home at that location (or maintenance of an apartment) or the continuance of activities at that place such as payment of taxes, membership in social and professional organizations, renewal of driver's and automobile licences, maintenance of a permanent mailing address, and maintenance of school registration for the taxpayer's children.

While the definition of temporary is a subjective one, the IRS considers a definite period of less than one year to be temporary unless contrary evidence exits.[27] The Service also will accept a definite period of one year or more if employment is expected to last less than two years and if, in fact, the employment does last less than two years provided the taxpayer returns to his claimed tax home after termination.[28] There is no support for a deduction if the length of employment at the new location is indeterminate or permanent. Thus visiting professors might find it advantageous to have the employment contract with the visited school specify a definite period of employment which is less than one year or in some cases two years.

Deductible travel expenses away from home include the cost of such items as transportation, food, lodging, and laundry. Since only the travel expenses of the professor are deductible, it will be necessary to allocate various items of cost when the family accompanies the professor. For instance, if the professor needs a one-bedroom furnished apartment but rents a three-bedroom

---

[26] For a more complete treatment of this issue see: Hreha, Taxes, May, 1985, pp. 333-339 and Henry, St. Louis University Law Journal, No. 4, 1982, pp. 779-811

[27] Revenue Ruling 60-189, 1960-1 CB 60

[28] Revenue Ruling 83-82, 1983-1 CB 45 amplifying Revenue Ruling 60-189, 1960-1 CB 60

unit because of the family, the deductible lodging cost is based on the cost of a one-bedroom apartment.[29] After December 31, 1986, such expenses will be treated as itemized deductions but only to the extent they exceed 2 percent of the professor's adjusted gross income. In addition, only 80 percent of the cost of meals will be deductible.

It is not permissible to deduct both travel expenses away from home and moving expenses. The professor may deduct travel costs associated with the trip to and from the site of the temporary position, but travel costs incurred by the family would not be deductible.

Typically, a visiting professor will rent his or her house to someone else while away from home. The rent received must be reported as gross income and expenses related to production of the rental income may be deducted. Deductible expenses related to the production of rental income may include advertising, transportation, property management fees, lawn care, property insurance, interest, property taxes, legal and accounting fees, maintenance, supplies, utilities and depreciation.

If the professor has any days of personal use during the tax year, total expenses must be allocated on a pro rata basis (based on number of days) between business and personal use. Personal use includes use either by the professor or a family member, unless rented at a fair rental price; another person with whom the professor has a reciprocal exchange of dwelling arrangement; or anyone else who pays less than a fair rental price. If the apportioned expenses exceed rental income, taxpayers will obviously want to deduct the loss from other income to determine adjusted gross income. There are two conditions which must be satisfied in order to do this.

First, the professor must establish that the residence was leased with the objective of making a profit.[30] The fact that the professor fails to lease the property profitably is not determinative of a profit-seeking motive.[31] If the professor fails to prove the required profit-seeking motive, the deductions will be allowed only to the extent of the rental income.

---

[29] Revenue Ruling 62-2, 1962-1 CB 9

[30] IRC Sec. 183 and Regs. Sec. 1.183-2(a) and (b)

[31] <u>Coors v. Commissioner</u>, 60 TC 368, 394 (1973), acq. 1974-2 CB 2

Second, the professor must avoid the vacation home rules.[32] Basically the vacation home rules provide that when the taxpayer or his or her family uses a dwelling unit for personal purposes for more than the greater of fourteen days or ten percent of the number of days the unit is leased at fair rental, a deduction limitation is calculated as follows. Rental income is first reduced by apportioned interest and apportioned real estate taxes. These expenses are deducted even if they exceed rental income. Remaining rental income, if any, is reduced by apportioned cash expenses such as insurance, maintenance, and other similar items. However, these expenses can only be used to offset rental income. Finally, an apportioned share of depreciation can be deducted but only to the extent of any remaining net rental income. Obviously, this limitation prevents any loss from being deducted against other income. This limitation does not apply if the professor rents or holds for rental his or her principal residence for a period of twelve consecutive months or if he or she sells or exchanges the residence at the end of that period.[33] Thus, in general, a professor who rents the home for less than twelve months will only be able to shelter the rental income. If the professor wishes to generate a deductible net loss, he or she must either rent the home for a consecutive twelve-month period, allow the home to remain vacant for the tax year in order to meet the 14-day or ten percent time test, or sell the residence at the end of the visitation period.

It should be noted that most taxpayers now deduct interest and property taxes related to their personal residence as itemized deductions. When the residence is rented, the apportioned interest and property taxes incurred during the rental period will no longer be treated as itemized deductions. Thus, some visiting professors may find that because of this reclassification of expenses from an itemized deduction to a deduction for adjusted gross income, it is no longer advantageous to itemize deductions. Because of this interaction, a visiting professor who intends to convert the personal residence to rental property, especially if the rental period corresponds closely to a calendar year, may want to consider the implications on the deductibility of other items such as state income taxes, professional dues and subscriptions, medical expenses and contributions. The visiting professor may find it more desirable to time these expenditures to correspond with a year other than the year when the professor is serving as a

---

[32] IRC Sec. 280A(d)(1)

[33] IRC Sec. 280A(d)(3)(B)

visiting professor.

Once the residence is converted to rental property, a deduction for depreciation on the house, but not the land, is allowable. If the professor elects to rent furniture, appliances, etc., additional depreciation deductions are allowed.

When property used for personal purposes is converted to business use, the depreciable basis of the property is the lower of fair market value on the date of conversion or the basis of the property at the time of conversion[34] usually cost. For a house, most taxpayers will probably use cost since it typically will be less than fair market value. After using the above rule to determine basis, it will be necessary to calculate the depreciation deduction. If the home was purchased after 1980 and before March 16, 1984, it should be depreciated using the 15-year straight-line method beginning in the month of conversion.[35] For homes purchased after March 15, 1984, and before May 9, 1985, the law requires a period of 18 years; for homes purchased after May 8, 1985, and before January 1, 1987, a period of 19 years is required; and for homes purchased after December 31, 1986, a period of 27.5 years is required. If the home was purchased prior to 1981, it will be necessary to estimate the salvage value and the expected remaining useful life of the home at the time it is converted to rental property. In view of the short time period and complexities of the depreciation computation, many taxpayers prefer to use the straight-line method of depreciation. However, it will probably be permissible to use the 125 percent declining balance method for the house and the 150 percent declining balance method for the furniture.

If a visiting professor decides during the visit to accept a permanent position at the visited school or possibly at some other school, he or she may no longer be considered as being temporarily away from home. Thus, only travel expenses incurred prior to accepting a permanent position will be deductible.[36] It is important to note that acceptance of a permanent job may make it more difficult for the professor to sustain the argument that he or she was originally away from home on a temporary basis.

---

[34] Reg. Sec. 1.167(g)-1

[35] IRC Sec. 168(b)(3)(A)

[36] Charles E. Hoffman, TC Memo 1971-120; Richard W. Beebe, TC Memo 1971-330; Israel Teicher, TC Memo 1972-41

CHAPTER VI

PROFESSIONAL EXPENSES AND REIMBURSEMENTS

Professors typically encounter a variety of expenses and reimbursements related to their teaching, research, and consulting activities which have special income tax consequences. It can be quite beneficial if both faculty and administrators are aware of these special tax provisions, since advance planning may help reduce tax liabilities. In some circumstances, proper administrative procedures can help the professor minimize taxes without any increasing cost to the university.

Special income tax provisions and certain recommended professorial or administrative actions will be discussed under the following headings:

(1) Reporting Requirements
(2) Transportation and Travel Expenses
(3) Educational Expenses
(4) Sabbatical Leaves
(5) Attendance at Symposia, Conventions, and Conferences
(6) Research Expenses
(7) Home Office,
(8) Personal Computers, and
(9) Miscellaneous Items

Reporting Requirements

To avoid repetition, general rules for treating income, reimbursements, and deductions in tax returns are summarized here. Specific reporting requirements are discussed in subsequent sections.

An employee who adequately accounts to his or her employer for expenses incurred on behalf of his or her employer and who is reimbursed for the exact amount of such expenses is not required to include the reimbursement in gross income, and accordingly, does not deduct the expenses on his or her return. Reimbursements in excess of expenses paid by the employee must be included in gross income. An employee who does not account to his or her employer or receives less than total reimbursement must attach a statement to the return which provides information on all reimbursements received and expenses incurred in order to deduct employee expenses.

After 1986 expenses are deductions from gross income (i.e., deducted in arriving at adjusted gross income) if they are attributable to trade or business (other than employee), rents and royalties, or reimbursed expenses of employees. The total of unreimbursed employee business expenses (except moving expenses, as discussed in a previous chapter), investment expenses, and certain other miscellaneous itemized deductions is eliminated to the extent of 2 percent of adjusted gross income.[1] The excess (if any), when added to other itemized deductions, provides a tax benefit to the extent the total exceeds the standard deduction.

Transportation and Travel Expenses

Transportation and/or travel expenses may be involved in many of the activities discussed in this chapter. General rules for deducting transportation and travel expenses are summarized in this section. Subsequent discussions in regard to these expenses are limited to providing more detail and discussing exceptions to the general rules.

Transportation costs related to business or for the production of income are deductible. These include transportation between job locations, transportation between clients' or customers' locations, and transportation from the office for the purpose of performing business tasks such as locating supplies, providing tours of the campus or city for prospective employees, and speaking to local groups or organizations.

Taxpayers may use the actual cost of operating an automobile for business or production of income, i.e., oil, gas, repairs, license fee, insurance, property taxes and depreciation, or annually deduct twenty-one cents a mile for the first fifteen thousand miles of business use and eleven cents for each additional mile. The mileage rate option may not be used if the taxpayer ever claimed accelerated depreciation/accelerated cost recovery system (ACRS) or bonus depreciation/expensing election for the automobile. In addition to the mileage rate, taxpayers may deduct tolls and parking fees.[2]

Deductible transportation expenses do not include personal commuting expenses such as trips from the professor's residence to the university. This is true regardless of the distance involved, the physical condition of the taxpayer, or the type of transportation used. Only in unusual situations, such as

---

[1] IRC Secs. 62(a) and 67

[2] Revenue Procedure 82-61, 1982-2 CB 849, as amended by Revenue Procedure 85-49, 1985-2 CB 716

transporting required tools, may a taxpayer deduct any part of the cost associated with commuting, and then the deduction is limited to the additional expense incurred for transporting the tools.[3] The Tax Court has refused to apply this exception for a professor's transportation costs even though it was necessary for her to transport teaching materials because she had no storage or work area at the college. The court found that the professor would have driven to work in any event and that she incurred no additional expense by carrying the books.[4]

Where an employee having only one employer is required to work at two different job locations in the same city on the same day, both the transportation costs of going from the first to the second job location and the costs of returning to the first job location are deductible. If the employee returns home from the second job location, the costs for transportation from the second job location to his or her home are considered to be commuting costs to the extent that they do not exceed the costs of transportation from the primary job location to the employee's home.[5] Employees will not be able to establish a second job location by establishing an office at home. A teacher who used an office in her home to perform teaching related activities was not able to deduct the cost of traveling to the military base where she taught typing classes.[6]

An employee who has two separate employers may deduct the transportation costs of going from the first job to the second job. A high school principal who also taught an evening class at the local university was allowed a deduction for transportation costs between the high school and the university.[7] If the employee returns home before going to the second job, the deduction is limited to the lesser of costs incurred or the cost of transportation between the two jobs.

While transportation costs generally refer to the cost of going from one location to another, travel costs include reasonable costs of transportation, meals, lodging and other

---

[3] D.W. Fausner v. Comm., 413 U.S. 838 (1973); Revenue Ruling 75-380, 1975-2 CB 59

[4] Ila Beards, TC Memo 1984-438

[5] Revenue Ruling 55-109, 1955-1 CB 261

[6] L.N. Kutchinski, TC Memo 1965-43

[7] D. Chandler, et al v. Comm., 226 F.2d 467 (1955)

expenses associated with the travel. In order for travel costs to be deductible, the taxpayer must be away from home overnight. To illustrate, assume that an employee, whose job location is in Anytown, is required to travel for business purposes to another town 125 miles away. If the employee leaves on Monday morning and returns that evening, only the transportation costs would be deductible. If the employee does not return home until Tuesday, the cost of meals and lodging, as well as transportation costs, are deductible. It also should be noted that when one is away from home overnight, transportation costs between the place of lodging and the business location are deductible, despite the similarity to commuting costs.[8]

Transportation costs similar to commuting costs are also deductible when one is required to report to a temporary work location instead of the primary job location. The IRS normally considers a job assignment of less than one year to be temporary (costs deductible) and of two or more years to be indefinite (costs not deductible).[9] For example, a professor at the University of Georgia in Athens who is required to teach full time in a continuing education program for three weeks in Atlanta, may deduct the costs of transportation to and from Atlanta. The importance of the temporary nature of the job must not be overlooked. If the job assignment were for three years instead of three weeks, it is likely that the job would be considered as either indefinite or permanent, making the transportation costs nondeductible.

In 1976, the IRS issued a ruling which sought to discard the temporary test for local and one-day travel and to establish a rule that transportation expenses incurred in going between the taxpayer's residence and place of work are non-deductible commuting expenses regardless of the temporary nature of the transportation, or the degree of necessity. However, the IRS has suspended the effective date of the this ruling indefinitely.[10] Recent Tax Court cases have been decided on the basis of the temporary-indefinite test.[11]

---

[8] Letter Ruling 8121050, February 26, 1981

[9] Revenue Ruling 83-82, 1983-1 CB 45

[10] Revenue Ruling 76-453, 1976-2 CB 86, as suspended by Announcement 77-147, 1977-42 IRB 45

[11] L.W. Norwood, 66 TC 467 (1976); R.E. McCallister, 70 TC 505 (1978); J.T. Allison, Jr., et al, TC Memo 1986-346

En route traveling expenses for domestic travel in the United States are not prorated; the full amount is deductible if the travel is primarily for business or the production of income. No deduction is allowable for en route traveling expenses if the travel is primarily for personal purposes. Costs at the destination directly related to business activities are nevertheless deductible; however, costs directly related to personal activities, such as sightseeing or personal entertainment are clearly not deductible.

For foreign travel outside of the United States primarily for pleasure, no en route travel cost is deductible. Such travel costs are fully deductible if the travel is primarily for business and (1) the trip does not exceed one week, (2) personal activities occupy less than 25 percent of the total travel time, (3) the taxpayer does not have substantial control over arranging the trip, or (4) a personal vacation is not a major consideration in determining whether to make the trip. For other foreign travel primarily for business but involving both business and personal activities, en route travel costs are deductible to the extent allocable to business.[12]

No deduction is allowed for travel expenses away from home unless the expenditures are substantiated. Unsubstantiated deductions prior to 1973 were guided by the Cohan rule, under which the courts made reasonable approximations and did not totally disallow the deductions. However, the regulations currently in effect specifically state that the Cohan doctrine has been superseded, and the Conference Committee Report underlying the 1986 Tax Reform Act reemphasizes that the courts and the IRS may not use the Cohan rule to allow deduction of a portion of unsubstantiated meal and other entertainment expenses. No relief from adequate documentation should be expected from the IRS; thus, adequate documentation should be maintained. Where travel expenses away from home are incurred, the taxpayer must prove: (1) the cost of transportation, meals and lodging, and incidentals; (2) the date of departure and return and the total number of days spent away from home on business; (3) the place or places of travel, including the name or location of each destination; and the business purpose(s) of the trip and the nature of the business benefit expected to be derived by the taxpayer.[13]

---

[12] IRC Sec. 274(c); Reg. 1.274-4; as an example, see A.F. Habeeb, TC Memo 1976-259

[13] Reg. Sec.1.274-5(b)(2)

Reimbursement arrangements, per diem allowances, and mileage allowances where in accord with reasonable business practices are treated as an adequate accounting to an employer or as equivalent to adequate substantiation for purposes of the procedures discussed immediately above.[14]

Taxpayers should be alert to the implications of not requesting reimbursement of expenses when such a right exists. If reimbursement is available but not requested, the nonreimbursed expenses may not be deducted.[15]

Special restrictions apply to deductions for luxury automobiles and luxury water travel. Also, after 1986 only 80 percent of certain meal and entertainment costs are deductible. Food and beverage costs incurred during travel away from home are included. Exceptions to the limitation include employee costs which are reimbursed by the employer or food and beverage costs included in the cost of certain qualified conventions, seminars, annual meetings, or similar business activities where such food and beverages are part of a program with a speaker.[16] In the case of the reimbursement, the effect is to limit the deduction by the employer rather than the employee (which, incidentally, does not affect tax-exempt institutions). Deductions related to income producing activities (IRC Sec. 212 expenses such as for investments) are no longer allowed for expenses allocable to a convention, seminar, or similar meeting[17]. Thus, to be deductible such expenses must be incurred in connection with a trade or business (including employee).

Careful planning and scheduling on domestic business trips can have added benefits. For example, if you are traveling on business and are accompanied by your spouse who is traveling for pleasure, you are allowed to deduct the amount you would have spent had you been traveling alone.[18] For example, if a double

---

[14] Revenue Ruling 80-62, 1980-1 CB 63, amended by Revenue Ruling 80-203, 1980-2 CB 101; modified by Revenue Ruling 84-51, 1984-1 CB 90 and amplified by Revenue Ruling 84-164, 1984-2 CB 63

[15] H.E. Podems, 24 TC 21 (1955); W.C. Stolk v. Comm, 274 F.2d 25 (1964); T.V. Orvis v. Comm., 788 F.2d 1406 (1986)

[16] IRC Sec. 274(n)

[17] IRC Sec. 274(h)(7)

[18] Revenue Ruling 56-168, 1956-1 CB 93

room costs $35 and single room costs $25, deduct $25 for lodging expense. Where single and double accommodations are priced the same, the full cost should be deductible.

When a spouse or other family member travels with the professor, tests will be applied for that person in the same manner as for the professor in determining whether the travel is primarily business or personal. Simply participating in business meetings, social functions, and/or discussions of business often is not sufficient to establish the necessary business relationships.[19]

Educational Expenses

Educational expenses are deductible if the education:

(1) Maintains or improves skills required by the individual in his or her employment or other trade or business, or

(2) Meets the express requirements of the individual's employer, or requirements of applicable law or regulations, imposed as a condition to the retention of an established employment relationship, status, or rate of compensation.[20]

Expenditures that maintain or improve teaching or research skills include refresher courses and courses dealing with current developments as well as academic or vocational courses. The costs of general education courses are typically not deductible.

Once the minimum educational requirements have been satisfied, one may deduct the cost of education which must be obtained in order to retain employment, status, or rate of compensation. An economics professor who met the minimum requirements for the position was informed in 1958 that he would have to obtain a Ph.D. or be terminated. His educational costs associated with obtaining the Ph.D. were deductible.[21]

Even though educational expenses may satisfy one of the above two provisions, the expenses will not be deductible if incurred to meet the minimum educational requirements for the individual's employment or will qualify the person for a new business.

---

[19] M.T. Weatherford v. Comm., 418 F.2d 895 (9th Cir., 1969)

[20] Reg. 1.162-5

[21] L. Robertson, 37 TC 1153 (1962) (Acq., 1963-1 CB 4)

The minimum education for an educational position is the aggregate number of college hours or degree normally required for initial permanent employment. Where no normal requirement (e.g., Ph.D. degree) exists in an educational institution, a professor is deemed to meet the minimum educational requirements when he or she becomes a member of the faculty. The particular practices of an institution must be considered, but he or she is generally considered to be a member of the faculty if (1) he or she has tenure or his or her years of service are being counted toward obtaining tenure, (2) his or her institution is making contributions to a retirement plan other than social security or a similar program, or (3) he or she has a vote in faculty affairs.

The fact that the individual is already employed does not establish that the minimum educational requirements have been satisfied. For example, if a person begins teaching at a university before finishing the dissertation and if the Ph.D. degree is viewed as the minimum educational requirement for a faculty member, such employment does not convert any remaining educational expenditures into deductible expenses.

When the education is part of a program of study which qualifies one for a new trade or business (e.g., a geologist taking accounting courses or a physics teacher taking law school courses), the cost of that education is not deductible. A teacher certified to teach in Canada moved to New Jersey and took courses which were required in order to be certified in New Jersey. Although the IRS disallowed the deduction on the basis that the education qualified her for a new [22] trade or business, the Tax Court upheld the deduction since the duties of both Canadian and New Jersey schools are basically the same.

A change of duties does not constitute a new trade or business if the new duties involve the same general type of work. All teaching and related duties are considered to involve the same general type of work. Also, educational expenses which enable one to obtain a promotion may still be deductible if the old and new positions involve the same general type of work. For example, a full-time lecturer in engineering at a college enrolled full-time at a university to complete requirements for a Ph.D in engineering before returning to the college as a lecturer in engineering. The Tax Court allowed the deduction because the expenses were incurred to maintain or improve his skills as a professor of engineering at the university level.[23]

---

[22] R. Laurano, 69 TC 723 (1978) (Acq., 1978-2 CB 2)

[23] M.V. Damm, TC Memo 1981-203

The IRS and the Tax Court generally hold that obtaining a law degree constitutes qualification for a new trade or business even though the person has no intention of practicing law. Accordingly, costs for obtaining a law degree are not deductible. The Tax Court has applied this rule to disallow education expenses claimed by a mathematics professor who pursued a juris doctor degree for the purpose of teaching law.[24]

Prior to the Furner decision, the IRS maintained that one could only deduct education expenses if employed at the time the expenses were incurred. In Furner the taxpayer resigned from a teaching position, entered graduate school in order to improve her teaching skills, and then accepted another teaching position.[25] The service now follows this decision allowing deductibility as long as the absence is not more than one year.[26] Courts have allowed more extended time periods when the person was actively seeking, but unable to obtain, such employment.[27]

Educational expenses include expenditures for tuition, laboratory fees, books, typing, supplies and similar items, plus costs of meals and lodging if the professor is away from home overnight. If the taxpayer attends classes which are held within the city or general area of the taxpayer's work, the cost of the one-way trip from work to class is deductible. The round trip transportation cost is deductible if classes are held outside the city or general area of the work. As discussed earlier for transportation and travel costs, beginning in 1987 qualifying unreimbursed education expenses are included in miscellaneous itemized deductions subject to the 2 percent adjusted gross income floor, and reimbursed education expenses are deducted from gross income if the reimbursements are included in gross income.

In some cases, an employer may have a tuition reimbursement plan whereby employees are reimbursed for educational costs if the courses are beneficial to the employer's business and taken with the employer's approval. When the employee adequately accounts to the employer and the reimbursement and expenses are the same, the employee is not required to report the expenses or

---

[24] K.G. Bouchard, TC Memo 1977-273

[25] M.O. Furner v. Comm., 393 F.2d 292 (1968)

[26] Revenue Ruling 68-591, 1968-2 CB 73; Revenue Ruling 77-32, 1977-1 CB 38

[27] R.J. Picknally, TC Memo 1977-321

the income.[28] However, this procedure may not be used when the employer's reimbursement plan is not limited to job related costs and the employee can choose any course he or she desires.

Prior to 1978, an employee who was reimbursed by his employer for non-job-related education expenses would include the reimbursement in gross income. However, for 1986 and 1987 it is possible for an employer to reimburse an employee for education expenses up to $5,250 under a qualified "educational assistance program" without the reimbursement being included in gross income. Such reimbursements can be made for job-related and/or for personal educational expenses. Payments with respect to any course or other education involving sports games or hobbies does not qualify. This special provision is currently scheduled to expire at the end of 1987, although previous expiration dates were extended.[29]

Sabbatical Leaves

Sabbatical leaves are often granted to professors to allow time to: (1) participate in formal study, (2) perform independent study or research, or (3) travel. In general, the first two categories involve education expenses which have already been discussed and research-related expenses which will be discussed in a later section. In addition to the normal expenses associated with education, a professor who takes a sabbatical leave may have to provide partially or fully for a substitute teacher. If so, those payments are deductible as miscellaneous itemized deductions subject to the 2 percent of adjusted gross income floor.[30]

After 1986 expenses incurred by a professor on a sabbatical leave for travel as a form of education are not deductible.[31] Thus, a professor of Spanish touring Spain to maintain general familiarity with the Spanish language and culture can no longer deduct the travel expenses. However, travel in connection with an activity that qualifies as a deductible education expense (discussed in a preceding section) or a deductible research expense (discussed in a later section) would be deductible under

---

[28] Revenue Ruling 76-71, 1976-1 CB 308

[29] IRC Sec. 127

[30] Revenue Ruling 76-286, 1976-2 CB 41

[31] IRC Sec. 274(m)(2); Reg. Sec. 1.162-5(d) overruled to the extent it allows deductions for travel as a form of education

these rules, subject to the limitations discussed in connections with the travel and education/research rules. For example, costs for the professor of Spanish to attend classes at a university in Spain in order to maintain or improve skills required in his or her teaching of Spanish would be deductible.

When a professor receives payments from his employer while on sabbatical, the payments will generally be viewed as gross income.

Attendance at Symposia, Conventions, and Conferences

It is normally necessary for a university professor to attend business and professional symposia, conventions, and conferences. Expenditures for travel to attend such meetings are deductible under the guidelines discussed in the prior section on transportation and travel expenses. For example, a chemistry professor was allowed to deduct cost of attending conventions for the purpose of keeping informed in his field, keeping in touch with other scientists, and advancing the interest of his university, even though he was not specifically required to attend the conventions by his employment contract and even though the university made no provision to reimburse him for the expenses incurred.[32]

Deductions by an employee for the costs of attending foreign conventions, seminars or similar meetings are subject to special restrictions and reporting requirements. Expenses of attending such a meeting held outside the North American area cannot be deducted unless the meeting is directly related to the active conduct of a trade or business and, after taking certain factors into account, it is "as reasonable" to hold the meeting outside the North American area as within it. Factors to be considered in determining "as reasonable" are the following: (1) the purpose(s) and activities taking place at such a meeting, (2) the purpose(s) and activities of the sponsoring organization(s), (3) the residences of the active members of the sponsoring organization(s) and at which other past and future meetings of the sponsoring organization(s) have been held or will be held, and (4) other relevant factors. In this context, the North American area is defined as the United States, its possessions, the Trust Territory of the Pacific Islands, Canada, and Mexico.[33]

Expenses of attending conventions, seminars, or other

---

[32] A. Silverman, 6 BTA 1328 (1927)

[33] IRC Sec. 274(h)(1)

meetings held on cruise ships cannot be deducted unless specific guidelines are satisfied. These guidelines state: (1) the cruise ship must be a vessel registered in the United States, and (2) all ports of call on the cruise must be located in the United States or its possessions. Also, a limit of $2,000 is placed on the amount which a taxpayer can deduct in any one calender year. The taxpayer claiming the deduction must attach two written statements about the cruise to the tax return. The first statement signed by the taxpayer must include information about the total days of the trip (excluding transportation to and from the originating port), and the number of hours per day devoted to business activity. The second statement must be signed by an officer of the sponsoring organization(s) and include a schedule of attendance at business meeting(s) including the number of hours the taxpayer was present.[34]

Registration fees and other necessary non-travel costs are deductible in arriving at adjusted gross income only if attributable to trade or business (other than employee), rents and royalties, or reimbursed expenses of employees. Other such expenses are included in miscellaneous itemized deductions subject to the 2 percent of adjusted gross income floor.

Research Expenses

In addition to the normal teaching and administrative duties, university professors are typically expected to communicate and advance knowledge by conducting research and publishing. Thus, expenditures associated with research conducted to meet employer expectations are typically deductible. Each professor has the responsibility for showing that the amounts claimed are reasonable and related to his or her particular area of competence.[35] Expenses for transportation, meals and lodging incurred by a university professor during a 10-month sabbatical leave for research were deemed to be deductible as ordinary and necessary business expenses.[36] However, one teacher was denied a deduction when she was unable to adequately relate her research to the duties of her job or to an expected economic gain.[37] In those situations where research activity is expected by the university, it might be helpful if this expectation were

---

[34] IRC Sec. 274(h)(2)

[35] Revenue Ruling 63-275, 1963-2 CB 84

[36] Revenue Ruling 74-242, 1974-1 CB 69

[37] T. Asta, TC Memo 1976-109

expressed in a written policy statement.

Prepublication costs incurred after 1975 in writing a book must be capitalized. After 1986 uniform capitalization rules require taxpayers to capitalize all direct costs, plus a "proper share" of indirect costs allocable to the book.[38] The Treasury Department is directed to write regulations implementing the new rules, and the Committee Reports refer to procedures in long-term contract regulations.

Costs capitalized prior to 1987 were amortized against revenues under the income forecast method.[39] The 1986 Tax Reform Act includes textbooks under inventory rules. If the deductions give rise to a tax loss, the "at risk" provisions limit the deduction to the amount that the taxpayer has at risk and can actually lose.[40]

Where research is undertaken with a profit motivation (e.g., textbooks) on a recurring basis, a professor should consider this activity a trade or business. Consulting also constitutes a trade or business. Related expenses are deductible from gross income. These expenses and related royalty, consulting and other such income are reported on Schedule C of Form 1040. Net income from a trade or business is subject to the self-employment tax. Advances against future royalties paid to an author are normally taxable to the author in the year of receipt. Loans from the publisher, as opposed to advances, should not be included in gross income.

The same expense incurred by a professor as an employee may receive different tax treatment than if incurred in a trade or business. For example, expenses incurred by a professor for scholarly research are deducted as miscellaneous itemized deductions subject to the 2 percent adjusted gross income floor unless reimbursed. The same expenses incurred in a trade or business of the professor are deducted from gross income and are not subject to the floor.

Home Office

Many professors maintain offices in their homes for study,

---

[38] IRC Sec. 263A added by the 1986 Tax Reform Act; **L.M. and S. Garrison**, 86 TC 764 (1986)

[39] IRC Sec. 280(b), repealed by the 1986 Tax Reform Act

[40] IRC Sec. 465

writing, consulting, or other professional activities. For concentrated efforts, seclusion often is sought away from the university office where interruptions and disturbances frequently occur. Perhaps the university office is inadequate for storage of books or materials needed or the university office is not always available. Deductions for home office expenses have been sharply restricted as a result of the 1976 and 1986 Tax Reform Acts. For home office expenses to be deductible, the home office must be used exclusively and on a regular basis:

(1) As the principal place of business for any trade or business of the taxpayer;
(2) As a place of business which is used by patients, clients, or customers in meeting or dealing with the taxpayer in the normal course of his trade or business, or
(3) As a separate structure which is not attached to the dwelling unit and used in the taxpayer's trade or business.[41]

The restrictions do not apply to certain items such as interest, taxes, and casualty losses which are allowable deductions without regard to their being connected with a trade or business or with an income producing activity.

To meet the exclusive use test, proposed regulations provide that a specific portion of the residence must be used solely for trade or business purposes.[42] It is not necessary that the portion of the residence be a separate room; a professor convinced the Tax Court that a part of his bedroom qualified.[43] Anything beyond a de minimis personal use will violate the exclusive use rule. The Committee Reports indicate that the "regular basis" test is not satisfied if the home office is used for occasional or incidental trade or business activities, even though the office is used for no other purposes.[44]

An employee who uses an office at home exclusively and on a

---

[41] IRC Sec. 280A

[42] Prop. Reg. Sec. 1.280A-2(g)

[43] G.H. Weightman, TC Memo 1981-301, holding against the taxpayer on other grounds

[44] House Report No. 94-658, 94th Congress, 1st Session 161 (1975); Senate Report No. 94-938, 94th Congress, 2d Session 148-149 (1976)

regular basis to perform school related work must also use the office for the convenience of the employer. In other words, a professor who wishes to deduct home office expenses as an employee must meet the "for the employer's convenience" test in addition to those described above. Factors for determining whether the office is for the convenience of the employer have not yet been specified. The employee may be able to support a deduction if the employer does not provide an office or possibly when the office provided is inadequate. For example, a college philosophy professor was entitled to deduct his home office expenses because his home, not his college office, was his principal place of business. The professor was employed by the college to do scholarly research and writing which he pursued in his home eighty percent of each working week. The Second Circuit Court of Appeals held that the professor maintained his home office for the convenience of his employer due to lack of adequate working space on campus.[45]

No deduction for home office expenses is allowed if the taxpayer uses the office in an income-generating activity if that activity does not constitute a trade or business. Thus, a taxpayer who uses an office at home to manage investment activities will not be allowed a deduction since those activities do not constitute a trade or business.

A professor who uses an office at home in connection with a trade or business separate from his or her job as a teacher must satisfy the tests above, and furthermore, his or her home office deductions are limited to the gross income derived from the operation of the home office trade or business and in applying this limitation the expenses must be considered in a specific order. This bars creation of losses from home office expenses to offset income from other sources. Proposed regulations specify that expenses deductible without regard to the home office rules (e.g., mortgage interest, taxes, and casualty losses) are applied against the gross income before other home office expenses, and the other home office expenses which do not represent recovery of basis (e.g., depreciation) are applied before those home office expenses which represent recovery of basis.[46] After 1986 all other deductible expenses attributable to the the trade or business not representing costs of the home itself (e.g., secretary's salary) must be considered in the gross income

---

[45] D.J. Weissman v. Comm., 751 F.2d 512 (2nd Cir., 1985)

[46] Prop. Reg. Sec. 1.280A-3(d)(3)

limitation.[47] Regulations that specify where this will go into the order have not been issued, but the Committee Reports seem to indicate these are applied before interest, taxes, etc.[48] Following is a summary of the order and limitations assuming the trade or business expenses consist of a secretary's salary, mortgage interest and taxes, utilities and repairs, and depreciation:

Order	Description	Limit on Deduction	Comment
(1)	Secretary's salary	Gross Income from the trade or business (GI)	
(2)	Mortgage interest and taxes	GI - (1)	Mortgage interest and taxes exceeding the amount deductible as trade or business expenses are included in itemized deductions (not subject to the 2 percent of adjusted gross income floor)
(3)	Utilities and Repairs	GI - [(1)+(2)]	
(4)	Depreciation	GI - [(1)+(2)+(3)]	

When allocating costs to the home office, any reasonable method of allocation (such as the proportion of total floor space in the house occupied by the home office) based on the facts and circumstances may be used. After 1986 expenses attributable to the trade or business conducted in the home office in excess of those that are deducted for that tax year may be carried forward.[49]

To illustrate the gross income limitation, assume a taxpayer qualifies for deduction of home office expenses as a consultant. He pays a secretary $1,000 and house expenses allocable to his business are: mortgage interest, $500; property taxes, $200;

---

[47] IRC Sec. 280A(c)(5)

[48] House Report No. 99-426, 99th Congress, 2d Session, Act Sec. 143 (1986)

[49] IRC Sec. 280A(c)(5)

utilities, $150 and depreciation, $400. If gross income amounts to $800, $800 of the secretary's salary is deductible as a trade or business expense, the interest and taxes ($700) are included in itemized deductions (not subject to the 2 percent adjusted gross income floor), and the remaining $750 ($200 of secretary's salary, $150 of utilities, and $400 of depreciation) may be carried forward. If gross income amounts to over $1,500, the secretary's salary of $1,000 is deducted as a trade or business expense, $500 of the interest and taxes are deducted as trade or business expenses, the remaining $200 of interest and taxes are deducted as itemized deductions, and the remaining $550 ($150 of utilities and $400 of depreciation) may be carried forward.

The tax basis for computing depreciation of a residence converted to business use is the adjusted cost or fair market value on the date of conversion, whichever is lower. A competent appraisal report covering the fair market value of the residence at the conversion point should be obtained.

A letter ruling may give some indication as to how the home office rules are to be applied. A teacher's assistant and wife, who was employed as a grade school teacher, used a room in their residence exclusively and regularly for employment-related activities. Each was required to perform certain job-related activities after normal duty hours, although the places of employment were not available after 5 p.m. The home office was used to prepare lessons, construct charts and learning centers, read educational literature, and file material and plans as well as for storage of educational texts, periodicals, slides, and files. The IRS ruled that, except for certain expenses such as interest, taxes and casualty losses which are deductible without regard to their connection with trade or business or income producing activities, no deduction was allowable for the home office expenses. The IRS concluded that the home office was not the principal place of business, was not used by patients, clients or customers and was not a separate structure from the dwelling unit. Apparently, the IRS did not find it necessary to reach a conclusion as to whether or not the "convenience of the employer" test was met.

In _Feldman_ the Ninth Circuit Court of Appeals (affirming a decision of the Tax Court) approved an ingenius plan to circumvent the restrictions on home office deductions. The court held that expenses for rental use are deductible for all bona fide rental agreements involving taxpayer's residence and that requirements for deducting home office expenses are not applicable when the rented property is a home office that is used exclusively by taxpayer.[50] Unfortunately, the <u>Feldman</u> results were overruled by the 1986 Tax Reform Act effective after 1986.[51]

Deducting home office expenses has tax implications upon sale or exchange of the property. The IRS has ruled that the gain attributable to the portion of the old residence used as home office will not qualify for rollover of gain on sale of principal residence.[52] In addition depreciation recapture rules would apply to the home office and the gain attributable to the home office would not qualify for the exclusion available for taxpayers age 55 or older.[53]

Personal Computers

If a computer is used exclusively at a regular business establishment its cost can be recovered under regular cost recovery (depreciation) rules or, optionally, up to $10,000 of the cost can be expensed under Sec. 179. For this purpose an office at home qualifies as a regular business establishment if (and only if) expenses of the home office are deductible.[54]

If the computer is not used exclusively at a regular business establishment special restrictions may limit the cost recovery deductions.[55] In such a case, an employee may depreciate the computer only if he or she can establish that it is used for the convenience of the employer and is required as a condition of employment.[56] In addition, the cost recovery method is restricted to straight line unless the computer is used predominantly (over 50 percent) for business.[57]

Recent IRS letter rulings indicate the IRS is taking a hard

---

[50]<u>I.S. and S.B. Feldman v. Comm.</u>, 791 F.2d 781 (1986)

[51]IRC Sec. 280A(c)(6)

[52]Revenue Ruling 82-26, 1982-1 CB 114

[53]IRC Sec. 121(d)(5)

[54]Reg. Sec. 1.280F-6T(b)(5)

[55]IRC Secs. 280F(d)(3) and 280F(d)(4)(A)(iv)

[56]IRC Sec. 280F

[57]IRC Sec. 280F(b)(2)

line on allowing deductions for home computers. Criteria included: (a) is purchase of the computer mandatory, (b) is an employee who does not use home computers for work professionally disadvantaged compared to those who do, and (c) is use of the computer required as a condition of employment? A college professor purchased a computer to conduct research and develop proposals for grants to support her research. The professor's employment was for only nine months. She had to extensively solicit grants support in order to continue her employment. A contemporaneous log was kept which showed the computer was used 100 percent for business. The IRS ruled that the computer was not for the convenience of the employer because (1) although work-related, it was not "inextricably related" to the proper performance of her job, and (2) there was no evidence that other employees who did not use home computers were professionally disadvantaged.[58] Whether use of the computer is required as a condition of employment depends on all the facts and circumstances. The employer need not explicitly require the employee to use the computer. Conversely, a statement by the employer that the computer is a condition of employment may not be sufficient.[59]

Another interesting effect may occur if an employee qualifies for deductions of both home computer and home office expenses. As previously discussed, deductions for home office expenses are limited to gross income reduced (after 1986) by all other deductible expenses attributable to the the trade or business not representing costs of the home itself. Thus, qualifying home computer costs may reduce the gross income limitation, thereby restricting current deductions for home office expenses.

Miscellaneous Items

A professor may claim as deductions the cost of supplies used for teaching or research activities, dues to professional societies and teachers' unions, as well as subscriptions to professional and technical journals and newspapers. The cost of a physical examination may be deducted as an employee business expense if such an examination is required by the employer.[60]

Cost and upkeep of uniforms and special work clothes are deductible if specifically required by the employer and not

---

[58] Letter Ruling 8615024, January 8, 1986

[59] Letter Ruling 8629060, April 24, 1986

[60] Reg. Sec. 1.162-6

suited for general use (e.g., graduation robes, protective clothes). Special accessories such as gloves and boots are also deductible.[61] For example, an art teacher was allowed a deduction for protective clothing smocks.[62]

It is customary for professors to deduct books as purchased, but the purchase of a large library in one year should be depreciated. A depreciable professional library, as well as depreciable furniture, professional instruments and equipment are tangible personal properties which, if they otherwise qualify, are eligible for and favorable cost recovery methods, including the additional first year expensing election.

Expenses for CPA examination review courses are nondeductible personal expenditures.[63] This concept has been expanded to deny a deduction for a bar examination fee.[64] A similar rule may apply for obtaining other professional certificates and designations. However, costs to maintain such certificates and designations may be deducted.

The IRS has ruled that when teachers go on strike in contravention of state law, and state law imposes a penalty on the teachers equal to the daily rate of pay, the amount deducted by the employer from the teacher's remuneration because of the fine must be included in the teacher's gross income. Furthermore, the amounts withheld by the employer as a penalty may not be deducted by the employee since no deduction is allowed for any fine or similar penalty paid for the violation of a law.[65]

Professors frequently receive complimentary copies of books from publishers to review for possible adoption. No income is recognized upon receipt of such books. However, if the professor donates the books to a non-profit organization and claims a charitable contribution, the fair market value of the books would be included in the professor's gross income. Thus, taxpayers who have itemized deductions less than standard deduction may want to

---

[61] R.E. Kennedy v. Comm., 451 F.2d 1023 (3rd Cir., 1972); Revenue Ruling 55-235, 1955-1 CB 274

[62] H. Kellner v. Comm., 468 F.2d 627 (2nd Cir., 1972)

[63] Revenue Ruling 69-292, 1969-1 CB 84; V. Archie, TC Memo 1978-425

[64] Revenue Ruling 72-450, 1972-2 CB 89

[65] Revenue Ruling 76-130, 1976-1 CB 16

avoid claiming a contribution deduction if such books are contributed to a charitable organization.[66]

No charitable contribution deduction is allowable for a donation of a future interest in personal property if the taxpayer retains a present interest in the property. Thus, no charitable contribution deduction was allowed for a professor who transferred title to a rare book collection to a state university library but reserved unto himself during his lifetime access to the books and the authority to permit or deny access to the books by others.[67] Also, the submission of an article to a scientific journal is not deductible as a charitable contribution, since it is not property which has any measurable value.[68]

Taxpayers may not deduct the value of services performed for a charitable orgranization. Even in a case where college professors volunteered their services to "project upward bound" and the federal government allowed the value of these donated services to be counted as part of the matching funds which the university was required to provide, no deduction was allowed.[69] Out-of-pocket costs such as transportation, telephone costs and supplies used when providing services may be deducted.

Charitable contributions are deductible as itemized deductions not subject to the 2 percent of adjusted gross income floor, while (after 1986) unreimbursed employee expenses are subject to the floor. Thus, to the extent amounts discussed in this section (see the preceding three paragraphs) are deductible as charitable contributions they are not subject to the floor.

---

[66] Revenue Ruling 70-498, 1970-1 CB 6; C.N. Haverly v. Comm., 513 F.2d 224 (7th Cir., 1975)

[67] Revenue Ruling 77-225, 1977-2 CB 73

[68] W. Fox v. Comm., 418 F.2d 511 (1969)

[69] C. Etheridge, TC Memo 1977-175

CHAPTER VII

OTHER FRINGE BENEFITS

Discounts and preferential purchasing arrangements potentially produce the most psychologically significant and perhaps the most administratively efficient means of channeling resources to the faculty. Various forms of retirement, medical care, and insurance programs typically make up the greater portion of faculty benefits, but these very important items are often taken for granted as a common denominator for all professions. As a result, the opportunity to acquire everyday goods and services at bargain prices looms as a visible and highly gratifying differentiation from other employments. Furthermore, except where the benefit is clearly structured as compensation for specific services, broadly based arrangements generally will flow through tax-free to the faculty member.

While the concept of providing benefits with before-tax dollars does create a lower net cost on the whole, there are several non-tax reasons for alternative compensation approaches. In some instances of excess demand (i.e., athletic events or parking where capacity is limited), a user cost serves to allocate the available supply. In other situations, the clamor for increased money compensation may be met in part by eliminating preferential faculty pricing in some areas, such as the bookstore, in order to generate more revenue to fund salary increases and to meet other operating needs of the institutions. These considerations, as well as others, bear heavily on the choice of a compensation policy. Lowest net cost is not always the controlling issue.

One significant problem with respect to providing non-monetary fringe benefits is the equitable distribution of these economic benefits to the most deserving. It is sufficient herein to recognize that allocation problems may exist as the institution seeks to bestow differential rewards to individual faculty members. Typically, the cost of these internally-generated benefits will be treated as one composite bundle available in various component mixtures to all faculty at some "average" amount.

Faculty Discounts

The opportunity for institutionally based employee discounts takes many forms, since academic institutions produce goods and services literally covering the broad spectrum of daily needs and wants. The most common discount source is the "company store" where books, supplies, and a host of personal, as well as professional goods often are available. Institutional printing and publishing facilities may price excess capacity at incremental cost to faculty. Recreation facilities and libraries often are available to the entire family. Faculty clubs and university-owned resort facilities are not uncommon. Child care and special training may be offered through programs in nursing, education, and home economics, as well as through the clinical practice facilities of behavioral study departments. Parking is a universal faculty need - always a problem but crucial for those universities located in urban centers. Student and faculty art may be rented at nominal rates. Surplus equipment from computers to automobiles can be sold to faculty members at advantageous prices. The stream of economic value from numerous educational institutions touches the everyday needs of faculty members in many ways.

In addition to those benefits available through the university, the economic clout of the institution often generates favorable price differentials to the university community. The university may negotiate group purchasing arrangements with common suppliers, and faculty discount programs through normal retail channels are common.

Housing

The value of lodging furnished to an employee by the employer is excluded from the employee's taxable income if the lodging is (1) furnished on the employer's business premises, (2) furnished for the convenience of the employer, and (3) the employee is required to accept such lodging as a condition of employment.[1] All these conditions are likely to be met only when the faculty member is on call such as required by medical school faculty with clinical oversight responsibilities or by faculty with custodial responsibilities such as dormitory supervision. University teaching and research assignments in remote or hostile environments may also qualify the lodging furnished to be excluded from taxable income. In the more ordinary arrangements, faculty rental housing may be provided at advantageous rates without triggering taxable income. Academic institutions frequently acquire residential property by gift or bequest. This property could even be converted to faculty rental property at advantageous rents or

---

[1] Reg. Sec. 1.119-1(b)

even sold to faculty members under attractive financing arrangements.

Before the TRA, the appropriate tax treatment of the rental value of faculty housing received was uncertain. Under prior law, some courts held that the rental value, in excess of the amount paid by the taxpayer, of the campus lodging was taxable to the employee.

The current provisions provide that income is imputed to the taxpayer only if the rent that is paid is less than 5 percent of the appraised value of the property. The appraisal would have to be performed by a qualified appraiser. Further, the rental value of the lodging for tax purposes is limited to 5 percent of the appraised value of the lodging.

One of the major obstacles encountered by new faculty members is the problem of securing financing for the purchase of a home. Often the university or college arranges with local financial institutions for the availability of mortgage funds. In certain cases, mortgage loans can be made from endowment funds. Another possibility for the university is to become a lender for faculty home mortgages.

As residential property costs continue to escalate more rapidly than faculty salaries, the university becomes more important as a source of apartments and homes available to faculty members under advantageous arrangements. Since housing represents a major expenditure for nearly every faculty member and since the university ordinarily can obtain funds at lower cost than individual faculty members, a school should be able to construct residential housing and lease to faculty members at fortuitous prices. The obvious conclusion is that such an arrangement produces a real economic benefit to the faculty member substantially greater than an equal cost to the school paid in salaries and consequently materially enhances the overall value of the faculty compensation package.

Tuition Plans

Educational institutions frequently provide some form of tuition plan for the family of faculty members. The nature of these plans may vary from remission or partial remission of tuition fees at the employing institution to outright grants of cash to cover tuition costs. The institution may offer the opportunity for lower tuition costs at other colleges and universities with which it maintains reciprocity. In some situations the employing institution will offer to pay all or a portion of the tuition for children of faculty members at any other like institution.

The TRA clarified the tax treatment of partial or full tuition reduction plans. Under the law, beginning after December 31, 1986, gross income shall not include any "qualified" tuition reduction. The law describes a qualified tuition reduction as a reduction in tuition granted by an educational organization to one of its employees for education below the graduate level at that or another institution. The recipient of the education may be either the employee or certain other individuals (e.g., retired employee, surviving spouse of a former employee, spouse of the employee, or dependent of the employee).[2] One important qualification to these rules is that the value may remain free of income taxation only if the tuition reduction program does not discriminate in favor of certain highly compensated employees of the educational organization.

Loans to Faculty

Loans to faculty members typically come from third-party financial institutions without direct ties to the school. However, there often are several sources of funds within the university system. The university may directly advance funds for travel, for research, or for personal needs under conditions involving repayment. Endowment and trust funds may be loaned to faculty members under terms not available from normal financing sources. Hopefully, the endowment fund fiduciary responsibility would not be impaired by a loan at less than market rates since the decline in income directly benefits the university. It seems feasible for universities to solicit endowment agreements which expressly permit the use of funds for loans to faculty members. In addition to loans of university-related funds, some schools cover various overhead expenses for employee credit unions in order to facilitate a lower-cost loan source and, at the same time, to encourage thrift by creating higher net returns to savers.

However, certain tax provisions[3] covering "below market rate loans" that were enacted in 1984 could reduce some of the benefits of the above financing arrangements. Basically, the issue at hand is whether a faculty member is required to recognize taxable income in situations when he or she has

---

[2] IRC Sec. 132(f)

[3] IRC Sec. 7872

received something of value (e.g., a below market rate loan) from the school in exchange for services rendered or to be rendered. If the value received from the school takes the form of a below-market interest rate loan based on the general rules of taxation and the specific requirements of Section 7872, and unless certain exceptions apply,[4] the taxpayer could be required to recognize income to the extent of the value received (i.e., the difference between the current Treasury rate and the interest rate actually charged). Thus, even though cash would not be received by the taxpayer, the law may require him to recognize the non-cash income received.

In such case, the provisions under Section 7872 would require the faculty taxpayers to recognize an amount of imputed interest income (i.e., in reality, the amount may be viewed as an additional amount of compensation) when borrowing money at below market rates. This imputed interest income is "fictitious" in the sense that the faculty member never actually receives anything tangible, such as cash; nonetheless, something of value which is taxable has been received.

However, to offset this inclusion of income, the taxpayer may be able to claim as an itemized interest expense deduction an amount equal to the imputed interest income. This interest expense would be deemed paid by the taxpayer back to the school, even though a cash transaction has not occurred. The deductibility would be allowed under current law as an itemized deduction if the loan proceeds are used to finance a first or second residence of the faculty member. However, if the loan is not secured by the taxpayer's home or second home, the interest expense would be only partially deductible as "consumer interest" through 1990. After 1990, none of the imputed interest would be

---

[4] If when the loan was made, the avoidance of tax is not "one of the principal purposes," then the imputation rules may not apply if compensation-related loans are $10,000 or less. Further possible support for exemption from the imputation rules is found in the Temporary Treasury Regulation 1.7872-5T(b)(11) in situations where the "interest arrangements do not have a significant effect on the Federal tax liability of the borrower or the lender." The provision provides exemption from the imputation rules in the case of "loans made by a private foundation or other organization described in Section 170(c) [such as a college or university] ... [if] the primary purpose ... is to accomplish one or more of the purposes described in Section 170(c)(2)(B) [organized and operated exclusively for educational purposes]."

deductible by an itemizer. Special rules are available for the deduction of interest expense incurred by homeowners for educational or medical needs.

If the faculty member does not itemize deductions and assuming that the proceeds are not used in a trade or business of the taxpayer, the interest expense would not be deductible. Hence, in such a scenario, imputed interest income increases the taxpayer's taxable income without any relief.

The above rules apply to term loans made after June 6, 1984. However, these rules apply for all demand loans, regardless of when made.

Professional Services and Other Fringe Benefits

The complexities of laws and regulations, the burdens of taxation, and the mysteries of the market economy create a need for specialists and technical expertise. Academic faculty members often require the services of professionals such as attorneys, accountants, family counselors, financial planners and investment advisors as well as others. These services may relate to business and investments for profit or to matters purely personal. As a general notion, the cost of professional services will be tax deductible if incurred for a business purpose or in connection with investments for the production of income. Those expenses that are incurred for the production of income are limited by a new provision added by the TRA.[5] Such expenses are deducted only to the extent that when aggregated with unreimbursed employee business expenses and other miscellaneous itemized deductions, the sum exceeds two percent of adjusted gross income. Fees relating to personal matters, such as the preparation of a will, ordinarily will not be deductible for tax purposes.

The university can arrange financial consulting, tax planning, and similar services without charge to the faculty or at a lower cost than otherwise would be available. When professional services or other fringe benefits are provided without charge, the employee may be deemed to have received taxable compensation equal to the cost of the service to the university.[6] If taxable compensation accrues to the employee, the employee also would have an offsetting deduction to the

---

[5] IRC Sec. 67

[6] Reg. Sec. 1.61-2(d)

extent that the professional service involved the determination of a tax liability, a matter concerned with earning or receiving taxable income from business or employment, or the management of investment property, subject to the two percent of adjusted gross income limit for deductibility mentioned above. Aside from the personal benefit to participating faculty members, the availability of competent professional advice and counsel allows the faculty member to direct more energy toward research and other academic pursuits and, therefore, may increase overall productivity.

Certain other fringe benefits often are included in an employee's compensation package by an institution. The general rule that governs fringe benefits is that any item that represents income to the recipient is taxable unless some specific provision in the law makes it nontaxable. Certain provisions of the law provide an allowance for partial or complete exclusion of certain fringe benefits.

Some of the types of fringe benefits that may be excluded from an employee's income tax calculation are:

1. The value of child or dependent care services provided by an employer to enable the employee to work. The amount excluded cannot exceed the earned income of either spouse. The type of services for which an exclusion is available is the same type that would be eligible for the Credit for Child and Dependent Care Expenses,[7] if the employee had actually incurred such costs.

2. Fringe benefits that are chosen from among a number of options that comprise a "cafeteria plan." The employee is able to choose cash compensation (which would be subject to taxation), or he or she may receive a nontaxable fringe benefit. Such "cafeteria plans" are available under Code Section 125 if the plan is designed following certain criteria.

3. Certain group legal services plans up to December 31, 1987.

4. Accident, health, and life insurance programs.

5. Those fringe benefits that are described in one of four

---

[7] IRC Sec. 129

broad classes of benefits.[8]

** No-additional-cost services are those benefits that are available to an employee if they normally are provided by the employer in the line of work engaged in by the employee and if no substantial costs are incurred by the employer in providing such benefit.

** Qualified Employee Discounts are discounts provided to an employee for goods or services within certain limitations. This benefit is extended to the spouse and dependents of the employee as well as to former or disabled employees.

** Working Condition Fringe Benefits are those benefits that are provided by an employer that may be excluded by employee if they would have otherwise been deductible had they been paid by the employee. The value of a parking space provided an employee, even though it does not fit neatly within the above definition, is an example of this type of fringe benefit.

** De Minimis Fringes are items that are so small that accounting for them would be impractical. Examples would be personal use of the employer's copying machine, the typing of a personal letter by the employer's secretary, and occasional social or recreational events funded by the employer. In each case, value has been received by the employee, yet the value of the items is excluded from taxation because of the administrative burden that would be required if the items were taxable.

With the exception of working condition fringes, these types of fringe benefits may not be offered by an employer so as to discriminate in favor of high ranking or highly compensated employees. If the distribution is discriminatory, the fair market value of the benefits are subject to taxation by the recipient employee.

Reporting of Fringe Benefits

As employee benefits have expanded, compensation in the form of fringes or perquisites has become more intricate and sophisticated. As long as the income is subject to taxation, employees will try to avoid the full tax by receiving some

---

[8] IRC Sec. 132

benefit in kind. Congress has expressly sanctioned some benefits such as group term life insurance, pension programs, and group legal insurance plans which escape taxation, either partially or fully. If Congress has not provided in specific language that an item may be excluded from income tax, its fair market value must be included in the tax calculation in the year of receipt.

Employee benefits are made available to increase the economic value of employment and, more importantly, to sustain employee morale and improve the motivation and psychic satisfaction of the employee relationship. A significant step in producing the desired result from any compensation and benefit plan is to communicate to the employee in a manner which provides an understanding of the extent and value of benefits available. This key step in the compensation and benefits program should receive the same initiative and direction applied to securing faculty benefits. The faculty can hardly be motivated by benefits which remain unrecognized or misunderstood.